Libby Hall
for "Vita".

How to Be
Your Dog's Best Friend

THE MONKS OF NEW SKETE

How to Be
Your Dog's Best Friend

A Training Manual for Dog Owners

Little, Brown and Company
Boston—New York—Toronto—London

Some material in this book appeared in *Off Lead,* the *National
Dog Training Monthly,* and in *Gleanings,* Journal of New
Skete, in slightly different form.

Text, photographs, and illustrations by the Monks of New
Skete.

LIBRARY OF CONGRESS CATALOGING IN PUBLICATION DATA

Monks of New Skete.
  How to be your dog's best friend.

  Bibliography: p.
  Includes index.
  1. Dogs — Training. I. Title.
SF431.M66 1978   636.7′08′87   78-8553
ISBN 0-316-60491-7

30 29 28 27 26 25

MV

*Designed by Susan Windheim
Published simultaneously in Canada
by Little, Brown & Company (Canada) Limited*

PRINTED IN THE UNITED STATES OF AMERICA

In Memory
of
Thomas Dobush,
Monk of New Skete

Acknowledgments

All trainers, whether or not they attend schools and clinics themselves, develop a great part of their philosophy and techniques through personal exchanges with others in the field. Many people have helped us through the years in both our breeding and training programs and we would like to make special mention of them here.

Several veterinarians are in touch with us on a regular basis through our mutual referrals and their active cooperation with us in handling problem behavior: especially Drs. Joel Edwards and David Wolfe, Shaker Veterinary Hospital, Latham, New York; Drs. Eugene and Jean Ceglowski, Rupert Veterinary Clinic, Rupert, Vermont; Dr. George Glanzberg, North Bennington, Vermont; Dr. Robert Sofarelli, Saratoga Springs, New York; and Dr. Charles Kruger, Seattle, Washington.

A great many professional trainers have helped us during their visits to New Skete or in many other ways: Joyce and Don Arner of Westmoreland, New York; Jack Godsil of Galesburg, Illinois; Fred Luby of the United States Customs Office in New York City; William Lejewski of the Baltimore, Maryland, Police Department; Sidney Mihls of Englewood Cliffs, New Jersey; and Diane Moorefield of Atlanta, Georgia.

For supplying invaluable source materials dealing with the whole spectrum of canine–human relations, we want to thank Dr. Benjamin Hart, University of California at Davis; Evelyn Mancuso of Natick, Massachusetts; and Lynn Levo, C.S.J., of the College of St. Rose at Albany, New York; and also the following whose general assistance and encouragement have helped to make this book a reality: Elizabeth Ryder and Marian Finke; Helen and Jack Dougherty; Alice Riggs and Marie Leary; Eva and Ernest Seinfeld; Barbie and Bill Fleischer; Roby and Charles Kaman; Gordon Johnson; Ilse and Tony Govoni; Holly and Paul Carnazza; Roger Donald, Richard McDonough, and Diane Muller of Little, Brown; Jody Milano; the Nuns of New Skete; and our many clients who have entrusted us with the care and training of their dogs.

Finally, there is no way that can adequately express our thanks and affection to Helen (Scootie) Sherlock, who has expended incalculable hours of advice, guidance, and encouragement in every phase of our life and work with dogs here at New Skete.

Foreword

This is a very special book. In fact, it is a unique and major breakthrough in the area of animal training. It rises above the usual "cookbook" texts of how to train a dog, by providing a wealth of insights that will help the trainer/owner understand, appreciate, and respect his or her canine companion.

As I have stressed in my own books on pets, *understanding* is the key to communication, compassion, and communion. The Monks of New Skete have combined such knowledge and sensitivity to create this practical guide to dog training. They first inform, sensitize, and educate the trainer/owner, which is an essential prerequisite: the teacher must be educated and enlightened before he or she can hope to develop the potentials in the pupil, be it canine or human.

A reverence for all life entails responsible stewardship as well: love is not enough. Understanding your dog and knowing how to control him, develop his potentials, and resolve behavior problems, emotional conflicts, and frustrations are no less essential than love and respect.

I enjoy the subtle ways in which the authors give practical advice on a variety of topics, from choosing a pup to obedience training and dealing with behavior problems. They present the advice in an easy-to-follow way, but not cookbook style. Rather, they make the reader reflect on human-centered values, attitudes, and beliefs, exposing many fallacies vis-à-vis the nature of dogs. The re-sult is that one gains insight as to the nature of the dog, its psychology, emotional needs, and behavior patterns. Human-centered perceptions and conceptions become dog-centered as they establish the very foundation for training: compassionate understanding. They call this "inseeing." To attempt to accomplish and convey this in a book is a monumental task, and they have succeeded admirably.

I am sure that the Brothers join me in acknowledging our debt to those who have taught us so much, namely our companion animals. When the human mind and will are stilled, and we simply observe our animal kin, we begin to learn from them. Such wisdom not only enriches one's life, it also, in a very practical sense, leads to deeper appreciation and responsible commitment.

Lack of commitment, irresponsible ownership, and lack of knowledge are behind much of the indifference, neglect, misunderstanding, and abuse to which dogs are subjected in society today. Animals can make us more human — that is, more humane, patient, responsible, and compassionate. This book by the Monks of New Skete is thus a significant contribution both to humanity and to our closest earthly companion, the dog. It opens a door in our hearts and minds so that we may enjoy and enjoin with a fellow-creature whose devotion, loyalty, trust, and honesty toward us is perhaps the closest thing in the animal kingdom to what we humans regard as "right living" in the religious sense;

and in a very practical sense, this book is also the key to a harmonious and satisfying relationship between dogs and their human companions.

MICHAEL W. Fox, D.Sc., Ph.D., B.Vet. Med., M.R.C.V.S., Director, Institute for the Study of Animal Problems Division of the Humane Society of the United States

Introduction

Today there is a strong emphasis on material accumulation and growth, yet man still finds himself cut off from his material and spiritual roots in the world, in nature. Obsession with money and status, fashion and fad, competition, achievement, and power is choking off the sources of renewal and peace, not only in our culture but within each of us. Without strong and nourishing channels to our environment and to the past from which we sprang, we will not only lose what balance we now have as a civilization, but also the passion to "go beyond ourselves," to reach out to new horizons.

From earliest history man and dog have formed a nonthreatening, constructive bond of emotion and communication. In what now seems an almost magnetic attraction, these two seekers for survival found a relationship that even today can cut through the artificiality of technological stresses. Our very senses have lost contact with the circuits that link us to the rest of nature — and to ourselves. By taking up again the age-old kinship between man and dog, we can begin to slow the pell-mell rush toward extinction not only of an "endangered species" but of man himself. When we lose the essence of our own life, we jeopardize all other life in our own death throes. The essence and survival of the dog itself lies in its sound relation to man.

Sharing your life with a dog entails more than the obvious companionship and affection. Though we often are aware only of "intellectual content" when we communicate, it is also important to understand the basic ebb and flow of relating in a human context, the transmission of sometimes contradictory messages through bodily posture and touch, voice tone, facial expression, and eye contact. Is it the sophistication of man's progress — or the resulting short-circuiting of his basic understanding — that has blocked these vital elements of "humane-ness" from his life? To begin paying attention to your dog can provide relief from self-preoccupation and enfeebling neuroses, from physical and mental confinement, and from pressures that impede our intuition, caring, and the lifting of man's spirit.

Your efforts to key into another being — your dog — to read its reactions and to register nuances of its behavior can heighten your ability to empathize. Trying to get a feel for the basic psychology and responses both of play and of daily exchange of thought and feeling with your dog should enhance your capacity to deal maturely with yourself and other human beings.

Honest and effective communication serves as the foundation for more advanced and constructive interaction. Experience together serves as a training ground for *both* dog and man, with each building higher levels of response and competence. "Training," of course, can be viewed from many standpoints — the outlook espoused by this very definitive book focuses on directing latent talents, on accepting the presence of your own potential, which proper rapport can discover and develop. Merely to use the dog as an extension of man's ego satisfaction, of his desire for more efficient machinery for often very selfish and shortsighted goals, implies the use of force and grueling routine to elicit a specific response. This can only result in the destruction of the balance and richness of the dog's potential and man's loss of another link with his own sources of creativity.

Complex levels of emotion and ego link dogs and owners — often a dog must compensate for a lack in the owner's past or present life. The dog becomes the owner's self-extension, to some degree. Dog trainers, breeders, professional handlers, boarding-kennel proprietors, veterinarians, and others whose life's work is with animals soon learn to respect the complex intertwining of owner/dog identities. Contending with this situation often calls for the fullest measure of patience and compassion. Persons working on a full-time basis with animals often glean an unusual quality of empathy through their own feedback and interaction with their living charges.

My own experiences over the years in breeding, importing, judging, training, and acting as lecturer and consultant in matters pertaining to dogs have brought me into constant contact with all strata of people. When I reflect upon these encounters, my contact as a consultant for the German shepherd breeding and training programs at New Skete stands out as the beginning of a time of singular exchange between myself and the monks and nuns of New Skete, and the myriad people and dogs touched through them. New Skete, as an integrated totality, is an ideal environment, and a life-style which neither challenges, qualifies, adds to, nor subtracts from nature's own harmony. There is about New Skete a special tone that reflects the community's inner tuning to *natural fundamentals* (not to be confused with "religious formulae"). Whether it is a dog touching base there or a person involved through the dog training, breeding, boarding, or consultant capacities offered there, each is consciously brushed by the atmosphere of seemingly effortless and elemental harmony at New Skete.

Those of us closely bound up with animals and gravely concerned about the future — of dog and man — can only hope that this book will touch some responsive chords, on a visceral rather than intellectual level. Perhaps it will promote a broader outlook made up of more concern for individual characteristics, more humane concepts, and a broader understanding of the relationships of living things, rather than the popular training cult's recipelike way of "dealing with a problem."

HELEN SHERLOCK
Caralon Kennels
Ballwin, Missouri

Learning the value of silence is learning to listen to, instead of screaming at, reality: opening your mind enough to find what the end of someone else's sentence sounds like, or listening to a dog until you discover what is needed instead of imposing yourself in the name of training.

— THOMAS DOBUSH, Monk of New Skete (October 9, 1941–November 7, 1973), *Gleanings*, the Journal of New Skete, Winter 1973.

I love inseeing. Can you imagine with me how glorious it is to insee, for example, a dog as one passes by. *Insee* (I don't mean in-spect, which is only a kind of human gymnastic, by means of which one immediately comes out again on the other side of the dog, regarding it merely, so to speak, as a window upon the humanity lying behind it, not that,) — but to let onself precisely into the dog's very center, the point from which it becomes a dog, the place in it where God, as it were, would have sat down for a moment when the dog was finished, in order to watch it under the influence of its first embarrassments and inspirations and to know that it was good, that nothing was lacking, that it could not have been better made. . . . Laugh though you may, dear confidant, if I am to tell you *where* my all-greatest feeling, my world-feeling, my earthly bliss was to be found, I must confess to you: it was to be found time and again, here and there, in such timeless moments of this divine inseeing.

— RAINER MARIA RILKE, *New Poems*, translated by J. B. Leishman

But now ask the beasts and let them teach you,
And the birds of the air and let them tell you,
Or speak to the earth and let it teach you,
And let the fish of the sea recount to you,
Which among these does not know that the hand of the Lord has done this,
In whose hand is the life of every living thing,
And the breath of all human beings.

Job 12: 7–10

Contents

An Introduction
to Training

1 Myths, Mutts, and Monks

It may strike the reader as odd to find a book associating monks and dogs. Well, both have been around for a long time. Dogs, we must say, have monks beat by many a century, for according to some legends they even predate man's creation.

Indian myths furnish the most ready examples. For the Kato Indians of California the god Nagaicho, the Great Traveler, took his dog along when he roamed the world creating. He is quoted sharing his delight in the goodness and the variety of his creatures with his little dog. Among the Shawnee of the Algonquin nation that once inhabited the upstate region of New York where our monastery is located, creation was brought about by Kukumthena, the Grandmother, and she too is accompanied by a little dog (her grandson tags along too). Creation in this myth is perpetuated by none other than this mutt, for each day Kukumthena works at weaving a great basket, and when it is completed the world will end. Fortunately for us, each night the dog unravels her day's work. Those of us who have lost portions of rug, clothing, or furniture to a dog's oral dexterity may never be convinced that that ability could be put to such a positive use as forestalling the end of the world, but still the myth is very telling about the interrelationship between dogs and humans.

The place of dogs in mythology is not by any means limited to North American Indian cultures. It appears to be universal. Greco-Roman literature features dogs in various roles. Think of Hecate's hounds, the hunting dogs of Diana, and Cerberus of Hades. Then there is Asclepius, god of medicine, who as an infant was saved by being suckled by a bitch. And of course, Romulus and Remus (to stretch a point). Egypt had her share of dogs in mythology, which appear prominently in wall painting, and many have come to us intact as mummies.

Persian mythology features a dog in the account of creation. The Aztec and Maya civilizations include one as well. Various tribes of Africa, the Maoris of New Zealand and other Polynesian cultures, along with the venerable traditions of the Hindu and Buddhist have all found some place for a dog in the legends that have been handed down in both oral and literary traditions.

Zen monks, for instance, are fond of dogs. Many Zen monasteries keep dogs, usually outside the gates. Stories about dogs abound in Zen literature. In one, a monk is caught in an ironical game of one-upmanship with a dog:

Once a Zen monk, equipped with his bag for collecting offerings, visited a householder to beg some rice. On the way, the monk was bitten by a dog. The householder asked him this question:

"When a dragon puts even a piece of cloth over himself, it is said that no evil

one will ever dare to attack him. You
are wrapped up in a monk's robe, and
yet you have been hurt by a dog: why
is this so?"

It is not mentioned what reply was
given by the mendicant monk.

And in another, a continuation of the
above story, the unpredictable nature
of some dogs is equated with reality
itself:

As he nurses his wound, the monk goes
to his master and is asked still another
question:
  Master: "All beings are endowed with
the Buddha-nature: is this really so?"
  Monk: "Yes, it is."
  Then pointing to a picture of a dog
on the wall, the wise old man asked: "Is
this, too, endowed with the Buddha-
nature?"
  The monk did not know what to say.
Whereupon the answer was given for
him. "Look out, the dog bites!"*

We should not want to short-
change the Judeo-Christian inheri-
tance that most of us share. But in
fact the Bible, for reasons we cannot
examine here, has only an occasional
mention (usually negative) of dogs.
However, as Christianity absorbed
folk tradition, the dog reappears,
sometimes as a symbol of faithfulness,
sometimes as a little detail that lends a
warm and human touch to the story
of a saint's life. Perhaps the most vivid
example of the penetration of folk
legend into Church tradition is the
story of St. Christopher. Many people
will be startled by the way he is pictured in the Eastern Church. He has
the head of a dog, but otherwise he

* D. T. Suzuki, *The Zen Monk's Life*
(New York: Olympia Press, 1965), p. 25.

*In iconography, Saint Christopher has
the head of a dog. Later he is turned into
a handsome brute.*

resemblés the conventional image of a
martyr, down to the cross in his hand.
The *Menaion*, or Book of Calendar
Feasts, includes a brief account of
each saint's life. We learn from this
book that Christopher was a descen-
dant of the Cynocephali, a legendary
race of giants with human bodies and
canine heads. He is pictured thus in
icons. He was miraculously converted

and baptized, and given the name Christopher, which means Christ-bearer. Many saints in the Orthodox tradition are called God-bearer or Christ-bearer as a salutory title meaning the saint carries God within, in a spiritual sense. In the Western Church the title was taken literally and the legend subsequently developed where the man (an unattractive giant still) carried the Christ Child across a flooded stream and was transformed into a handsome brute instead. In the Eastern tradition he journeyed to Syria to attempt to make an evil pagan king, Dagon by name, see the light. The king was not impressed, even by so formidable a messenger as a dog-faced man. Christopher was imprisoned instead, and in the midst of his martyrdom (he was given the first hot seat on record: Dagon ordered him to be chained to an iron throne and then had a fire built under it — so hot, it is recorded, that both chain and chair melted) he was transformed and received the face of a man.

There is a story, perhaps still told in Roumania where it is thought to have originated, that gives a charming account of how the dog himself was created.* It seems St. Peter was taking a stroll in heaven with God when a dog came up. "What's that?" said St. Peter. God told him it was a dog, and he added, "Do you want to know why I made him?" Naturally Peter was interested. "Well, you know how much trouble my brother, the Devil, has caused me . . . how he made me drive Adam and Eve out of Paradise.

* Maria Leach, *God Had a Dog* (New Brunswick: Rutgers University Press, 1971).

The poor things nearly starved, so I gave them sheep for meat and warm wool to clothe them. And now that fellow is making a wolf to harry and destroy the sheep! So I have made a dog. He knows how to drive the wolf away. He will guard the flocks. He will guard the possessions of man."

Historically, two groups of monks have been responsible for breeding and training dogs. The canons of St. Augustine (technically not monks, but members of a religious order) have raised St. Bernards at the hospice in the Swiss Alps for more than two centuries. The dogs are still bred at the hospice, although they no longer perform their well-known rescues of travelers lost in the Pass — airplanes and snowmobiles have limited the need for the dogs in that capacity. But occasionally, the canons and their dogs do go out on a search. The famed brandy cask is a myth. It probably began due to the fact that the lost traveler, once found, was usually offered brandy by the Brother who accompanied the search dog. But the Brother carried the brandy, not the dog.

In Tibet, quite a different group of monks developed the Lhasa Apso dogs. They raised them in their monasteries and frequently gave them as gifts to nobles. It's interesting to note the disparity in size between these two monastic breeds, and the fact that two quite dissimilar groups of monks found working with dogs a fitting monastic occupation. We can attest to the experience that raising and training dogs fits into monastic life very well. Dog care takes a lot of labor and affection, and monks usually have both in abundance. On another level, the dog typifies in many ways the mature monk: loyal, steadfast, willing to please, willing to learn.

Monks should not be judged by the stereotype that no doubt rests in the back of the minds of many — the type with bowed head and folded hands, flowing single file down a medieval cloister corridor. Nor does the "Friar Tuck" image apply, though good nature, appetite, and a bellicose streak will be found to varying degrees in most monks. Actually, the best image to capture what a monk is can be found in the words of Dostoevsky, who remarks in *The Brothers Karamazov* that a true monk is nothing more than what all men ought to be.

Still, that is certainly debatable: "*What all men ought to be.*" Obviously celibate is not the answer. We have learned here at New Skete that the answer is never simple, and that sometimes there is indeed *no* answer. But there are many clues, and in our experience we have found that some of them have been provided by our *dogs*. They can in many subtle ways show us how we ought to be. They can show us how we ought *not* to be

as well. Dogs, because of their association with humans, an association that the stories we mentioned above show to be as old as human consciousness itself, are in a unique position to offer man a mirror of himself.

Anyone who knows someone with a pet will not have to search too far to find similarities between the two, in little things, perhaps, in behavior quirks, in outgoing friendliness, or in the opposite, suspicious reserve, and even — and often the most amusing — in appearance. Some cartoonists (such as Booth and Price in the *New Yorker*) get a lot of mileage out of the latter fact. By taking a closer look at all this, as in a mirror, we have found much to learn about our own behavior. And so we are offering our experience with dogs not just for the benefit of your dog, but in the hope that you, too, might learn something about yourself *through* your interaction with your dog. A better insight into your dog may give you a glimpse of your own humanity, and what is just as important, it should heighten the sense of responsibility we as humans have, not just for our fellow-creatures but for each other and for all creation.

2 How New Skete Went to the Dogs

In Egypt, there is a devoutly religious tribe called the Nuer. The Nuer live near the Nile River and raise cattle for their livelihood. But their cows

Brother Job with Zanta, a New Skete shepherd. (Photograph by Holly Carnazza)

are more to them than just a source of income. Barns, cow halters, and electric fences are foreign to the Nuer. Instead, they integrate their cows into the total fabric of their daily lives, utilizing them in work, letting them mill around, sleeping near them, and meticulously grooming and bathing them. Each cow has a name and a personal history, known by all the tribe. Daily life is characterized by incessant conversation (or so it seems to an outsider) about the cattle. Each tribesman has plenty of stories to tell about his cows, cows he has owned, or cows he hopes to own. The Nuer are always looking for the "ideal cow." Cows even attend some religious services, and Nuer ritual is full of references to you know what. Nuer religion has been studied extensively and is considered by anthropologists an archetypal primitive religion. The Nuer are, on the whole, physically healthy and psychologically wholesome. They live totally integrated with creatures of another level of existence.

Now, what has this to do with the training and breeding programs at New Skete? In some ways our lives at New Skete resemble those of the Nuer, and so we can appreciate many parts of their culture. We, too, consider our animals more than a mere source of money. We divide our training and breeding dogs among the Brothers. Each dog has a personal master or trainer. This handler comes to know the dog intimately. We shuffle around elements of our life to include the dogs on many levels. We try to make room for the dogs not only on a physical level, but in our

The monks sit down to dinner, with their dogs on down-stays near the table.

minds as well. It is very important to make room in your mind for other living beings. Whether primitive native or "civilized monk," raising a herd of cattle or a herd of dogs, it is a mind-expanding experience.

FIRST STEPS

New Skete monastery is in the hills outside Cambridge, New York, near the Vermont border. Early in our community experience, from 1966 to 1969, we had a full-scale farm. At one point or another, goats, chickens, pigs, pheasants, Herefords, Holsteins, and sheep all dotted our landscape. Without realizing it at the time, we were beginning to enter the psychic realm of animals. Our observation of the different farm animals began to educate us, on a grass-roots level, in animal psychology and behavior. We had a German shepherd dog and had thought about eventually breeding. Meanwhile, the farm animals were an excellent preparation for us. In a sense, training and raising German shepherds is the apex of our long experiences with animals. Our farm had to be phased out, since the new property we moved to, high on Two-Top Mountain, could not sustain a farm. We then made the decision to enter professional breeding and training.

Brother Thomas Dobush, who died tragically in an automobile accident in 1973, had an eye out for breeding and training programs as early as 1966, when "Kyr," our first German shepherd, insisted on coming with us from our former monastery. "Kyr" was a male, a former Seeing Eye stu-dent, and a volatile and intelligent shepherd. Later it was decided to purchase a bitch and plan a litter. From the beginning we studied our breeding and training plans carefully. We acquainted ourselves with any and all information on the subjects we could find. We contacted prominent breeders and trainers, asking for advice and counsel. Professionals recognized our sincere interest and desire to learn, and shared their knowledge with us. Similarly, we have always been happy to share our knowledge and experiences with novices. We are all beginners, in a sense, and we have found a learner's stance to be beneficial in increasing our knowledge of training and breeding.

Training dogs grew organically out of our experiences with our own dogs. Brother Thomas began training the shepherds to live in the monastery as a group and maintain quiet and order, important to monastic life. Later, our skills appealed to owners of other dogs, and we began to train all breeds. When a new monk entered, he was apprenticed to Brother Thomas and learned training skills. More than merely instructing his apprentices in handling skills and techniques (at which he was an expert), Brother Thomas tried to communicate an intuitive way of dealing with dogs. He emphasized "listening" to the animal and "reading" the dog's reactions. His training and handling skills were passed on in an oral tradition that is still alive at New Skete.

We live in a communal situation along with our dogs. The dogs live in a colony of upwards to twenty animals, of different ages and tempera-

A view of the main kennel building at New Skete.

An aerial view of the monastery and church.

ments. In general, our breeding dogs and training dogs do not mix extensively but do have some contact. Many training students are brought into the house. We limit the number of students we take at any one time, so that each dog can enjoy personal attention. We have taught obedience classes, but we feel more comfortable with a more individual approach. We live in a monastic situation where usually a quiet, reflective environment must be maintained. This quiet, we feel, helps humans and dogs to learn better.

As in the case of neighboring Egyptian tribes wanting to have Neur-quality cattle and learn Neur techniques, so too have we, by example and exposure, found people knocking on our door for advice. We always feel honored when clients ask for our dog-training or breeding skills. We consider each dog we train or breed a reflection on our monastery. What we produce is an indication of our integrity as trainers and breeders, and as monks who live with dogs.

3   What Is a Dog?

Dogs and men have been together as close companions for the last ten thousand years, if not longer. The origin of the domestic dog is still somewhat unclear. We know, for example, that when men and dogs began to live together, the only other animal with comparable dental characteristics was the wolf. The wolf is certainly the dog's ancestor, but he may not be the only ancestor. Most authorities believe that the dog is directly descended from the wolf, while others subscribe to a modified theory that teams up the wolf with some other close relative, who may have looked more like a dog. The evolution of different breeds is a fascinating study beyond the scope of this book. For those interested in training or just in becoming better friends to their dogs, one fact is important to remember: every dog claims the wolf as an ancestor. Understanding wolf behavior will help you to understand your dog.

There is still a great deal of prejudice against the wolf. Today it surfaces when environmentalists and others clash with those who believe that wolves deplete the deer population and attack livestock and even small children. (The fact is, the wolf can aid deer survival by eliminating the weaker members of a herd.) Since the wolf is a pack animal, it is sociable with its own kind but wary of humans, unless raised in captivity from a young age. Many people confuse the hunting habits of the wolf with those of the fox. Though the wolf moves pretty much with the pack, the fox is a solitary hunter. Wolves invariably stay as far away from humans as possible. Unfortunately, prejudice against the wolf thwarts a possible way of appreciating the dog, since wolf and dog have striking similarities. Both are innately pack-oriented and prefer not to be isolated for long periods of time. Both are hunters who chase down their prey instead of ambushing it like some of their other close relatives. Both are responsive to leadership from an "Alpha-figure" to whom they look for order and directives. Both use a wide array of body language to communicate within the pack and with outsiders. Some researchers have noted the presence of a kind of altruistic love in wolf packs, the willingness to please another member of the pack without any reward, and the ability to show caring. These last two traits are well known in domestic dogs.

To learn about dogs, learn about wolves. Books abound about *Canis lupus*, and they will provide you with invaluable background about your dog and its behavior. Some are listed at the end of this book. Reading about wolves in order more fully to understand your dog and its behavior is not going the long way around the mountain. If you reflect on the behavior of wolves, as reported in these books, you will discover an ironic fact: many books on wolves will help you to understand and appreciate your dog's behavior better than some of the dog-training manuals currently available. Many of the techniques in this book dovetail with what we know about the dog's close ancestor, the wolf.

Today's dogs belong to the family *Canidae*, along with their relatives, the wolf, coyote, jackal, and fox. This family of animals is remarkably diverse, but all members are carnivores, all hunt for food, whether alone or in a group, and all are potentially trainable and tend to learn easily, if raised in a human environment from an early age.

4 Some Important Terms

THE PACK

When we talk about the pack in this book, we usually mean the immediate members of the dog's social circle, both human and canine — in short, the dog's owner and those who live with the dog. Sometimes we will refer to this as the "family-pack." As previously mentioned, all dogs from the tiniest Maltese to the Great Dane have the wolf as an ancestor and wolves are pack animals. Since we have deprived the dog, through domestication, of its normal pack life, the dog has adopted us as its new pack. A dog perceives the people it lives with as fellow-members of a pack. Once a dog owner understands this, he can understand training methods that, while including the dog in the pack, lower the dog in the pecking order.

THE ALPHA

Within every wolf pack there is a leader, or Alpha-wolf. This wolf keeps order within the pack. The Alpha settles disputes between other wolves and may run interference for younger members of the pack. Depending on the individual pack, the Alpha's role might be one of dictator or guide, or he might adopt either of those roles at different times. All subordinate wolves look to the Alpha-wolf for direction. Domestication has not completely nullified in the domestic dog this desire to lead or be led. The problem comes when an individual dog does not receive proper guidance, through training, and fancies itself to be the leader, or Alpha. For a dog, there should be no question about who is the Alpha-figure in its life — you are. The owner must act as the leader, not because the owner wants to boss around a subordinate creature, but because

the dog is looking for direction and it is the dog's just due.

EYE CONTACT

One way the Alpha-wolf keeps order in the pack is by making eye contact with offending members. A piercing glance can often stop a fight from developing and settle disagreements. A kind glance can signify acceptance. We emphasize eye contact in this book because we feel it is an integral part of the way dog and owner should relate. It can prevent behavior problems from developing and stop them if they do. Assuming no behavior problems exist, eye contact between dog and owner can help to deepen their relationship, since it helps the dog to feel accepted and increases its trust in the owner. By eye contact used positively we mean gentle looks, not threatening stares. Used negatively, eye contact should be hard, penetrating, and sustained. But before the dog can read your eyes, it must look up at you. The techniques in this book encourage the dog to look up, so that eye contact can be made, whether it is in a positive or negative way.

TRAINING

The concept of training as we understand it in this book begins when the puppy is born. We do not treat training simply as a set of exercises (heel-sit, sit-stay, down, down-stay, and so on) that are imposed on the dog when it has reached a certain age. Instead, we approach training as a way of relating to your dog. We will treat

An example of eye contact with a young puppy.

many different types of activities as training, even though we emphasize the traditional exercises. Training, then, happens on many levels in a dog's life – not just in obedience school. J. Allen Boone put it well in *Kinship with All Life:*

If you would understand this secret, you must first understand the distinction be-tween *training* an animal and *educating* one. Trained animals are relatively easy to turn out. All that is required is a book of instructions, a certain amount of bluff and bluster, something to use for threatening and punishing purposes, and of course the animal. Educating an animal, on the other hand, demands keen intelligence, integrity, imagination, and the gentle touch, mentally, vocally, and physically.[*]

5 Selecting a Puppy or Older Dog

WHAT BREED?

If you are considering buying a pure-bred, you probably already have specific breed preferences. As you get ready to purchase a dog, you might review whether the particular breed you like is suitable to your environment and personality. The best way to find out is to talk to someone who has a dog of the breed you are considering. Almost every breed has a national breed club, and these organizations will be happy to level with you about the attributes of their breed. The American Kennel Club, 51 Madison Avenue, New York, New York 10010, can provide you with a listing of national breed organizations. Some popular books (Roger Caras's *Pet Book* is a good example) provide detailed breed descriptions. As for which breed is most trainable, we have our definite opinions, but no pat answer is possible. Many people with minimal exposure to dogs are full of set opinions about certain breeds. For instance, many German shepherd breeders or fanciers are "Shepherd Chauvinists" – to them no other breed exists, and German shepherds are the most trainable, since they are used for a great variety of work. A beagle lover will confess that beagles like to dig, but *never* bite, chew, or house-soil. Subtle or not-so-subtle prejudices emerge whenever the in-telligence level of different breeds is discussed.

Any opinions you may hear should

[*] J. Allen Boone, *Kinship with All Life* (New York: Harper and Row, 1954), p. 44.

A dramatic example of canine growth. Before you bring it home, be sure you know how big your puppy will get to be.

be qualified with direct experience with that breed. Remember that some breeds might have a tendency to exhibit certain behavioral traits, but it is usually the environment in which the dog lives that hides or heightens these traits.

MALE OR FEMALE?

Just as the potential owner usually has definite breed preferences, he or she usually leans toward one sex or the other, sometimes for the right reasons,

sometimes for the wrong ones. If it is difficult to express any solid opinions about different breeds and their characteristics, it is harder still to make flat-out statements about male or female characteristics. In one breed, the females might be docile and pliable. In another, they can be domineering and hard to control, although this is the exception. In general, we usually counsel novice dog owners to start with a female.

Females are often more resilient, smaller than males, and more easily trained at an earlier age. In many breeds, there is no appreciable difference between the protection potential of a male or a female; in others, the males are defensive, but the females tend to wilt in the face of danger. Specialists in different breeds will have more detailed information. Don't let a breeder pressure you into buying a male or a female, but if the breeder honestly suggests one sex over the other and seems to assess your situation correctly, it is a good idea to take the advice. The breeder probably knows more about your chosen breed than you do and is interested in making a good match between you and your puppy. No good breeder will place a puppy simply on the basis of sex.

Spaying (hysterectomy) should not dissuade you from purchasing a female. The spay operation is usually uncomplicated, and in some urban areas the services of a spay or neuter clinic are available. For that matter, some male dog owners will need to consider neutering their pets, especially as the pet population problem increases. Spaying can often have highly desirable behavioral side effects. While the fabled weight gain of spayed bitches is more fantasy than fact, behavioral changes usually do take place. Many dog owners report a mellowing in their spayed bitch, more responsiveness, and better retention of commands.

Don't choose one sex over the other because you want to get a male or female first and breed it with a second dog later. These plans may never materialize, unless you are definitely committed to starting a breeding program. Each dog should be selected on his or her own merits, not as part of a future breeding team. There is also the possibility that either partner may not turn out to be breedable, for a variety of reasons.

As previously mentioned, there is usually a personal preference in selecting male or female. There are some very prominent characteristics in the male of the species. However, we must bear in mind there is always the exception to the rule. But, on the whole, males tend to be more high-spirited, more in command of the situation, and in spite of their size — from the smallest poodle to the majestic shepherd — they have a manner of being aware of who they are and where they are, and not just what belongs to them — even without staking out their territory. Regardless of size, many can accommodate themselves to an apartment or country mansion. Their greatest need is their owner and they relate to him physically, psychologically, and emotionally. Pleasing their owners becomes almost their reason for being. Brother Thomas, who began our breeding and training programs at New Skete, once wrote, "We are to listen to a dog until we discover what is needed instead of imposing ourselves in the name of training." Male dogs have much to relate to the owner who takes the time to listen.

The following is an excerpt from a letter from a doctor and his family who had a New Skete male shepherd named Azzo. The letter was written after the dog's death, but the essence and spirit of the male of the breed has been captured beautifully.

His devotion was an example, and his restraint. He conversed continuously in silence and displayed a sense of humor and playfulness without which man would be unbearable. His imagination was a joy; his defense of "his" children was so ferocious that he turned robins and paper bags into dragons. Bees were monsters to be attacked, and he consumed more than were good for him. And never in his short life did he have any understanding of his size. His intelligence and selflessness and sensitivity were a challenge. He expected us to be wiser than he was and where reasoning was superior, we could be, but in all else he led us and made us better. His acceptance of our failures and weaknesses made us humble.

WHERE TO GET A DOG

The best place to get a puppy or older dog is from a reputable breeder. This breeder should be responsible enough to make a guarantee of temperament and health as well as providing the appropriate health information, a pedigree (if the dog is a purebred), and an AKC registration slip. Puppies or older dogs purchased from breeders are sometimes more expensive than dogs purchased from pet shops or puppy mills. But the extra cost is well worth it, even if you need to save to get your dog. Because of the conditions under which dogs live in pet shops, proper socialization often does not take place. Given that dogs are pack animals, the row on row of caged puppies does not seem an acceptable environment and substitute for early growth in a litter/family. Our experience suggests that behavior disorders in later life can result from improper socialization and suggest that pet shops be avoided in your search for a pup. When you buy from a breeder you gain the fringe benefits of his or her knowledge and advice for the future.

GETTING A DOG FROM THE ANIMAL SHELTER

In general, our advice to buy from a breeder applies here too. While the local animal shelter might be a source of potentially enjoyable pets, there are certain risks involved in selecting an animal from this source. Our case histories of dogs with behavioral problems show that a great many come from animal shelters. Often they were taken to the shelter precisely because they caused problems, and the frustrated owner decided to dump the dog in the lap of the animal shelter. Unfortunately, in many cases, all that happens is a simple transferral of the problem dog from one environment to another. Simply changing the environment cannot change bad behavior. It can sometimes help, but uprooting the dog and hoping it is placed in a country home or some other "ideal" situation is unfair to the dog and to the new owners. This is especially true of dogs that perceive of themselves as the Alpha or leader. Unless their behavior is modified by training, these dogs will tend to act as leaders no matter where they go. In short, dogs in animal shelters are sometimes problem dogs.

One might wonder if a young puppy obtained at a shelter would be a potential problem. Most animal

A loving mother. Try to see the sire and dam of the litter if possible.

shelter puppies are innocent victims. Perhaps they were the result of an unplanned breeding, and subsequently brought to the shelter. If so, there is a good chance that they were brought to the shelter before or during the "fear period" when they are particularly susceptible to stress and neglect. Many novice owners of unwanted litters wean their pups too soon, usually around the third or fourth week. The puppies begin to produce large, noxious stools as they begin to eat solid food. At this point, the litter becomes a burden rather than a joy, and the puppies begin to lose their appeal. If the litter was bred so that the kids could see "the miracle of birth," the pups are no longer useful. Then it's off to the local shelter with any pups that have not been sold or given away. Since there is usually no way animal shelter personnel can socialize the great number of youngsters they receive, the puppies are usually neglected at a critical time. Furthermore, since the act of taking a puppy or older dog to a shelter represents an alternative to caring for the animal, dogs at the shelter are likely to have been underexposed to important experiences and to have suffered from neglect before they entered the shelter. All of this makes for a very risky situation if you opt for selecting a pet from a shelter.

If, however, you still decide to choose a pet from a shelter, the information we present might help you to do it in a more informed way and offset the chance of taking home a potential problem. First, inquire with shelter personnel about the background of the animal. Did it live in a family? Has it been exposed to children, noise, stairs, city life? Why was it brought to the shelter? When you view the dogs themselves, try to "read" each dog individually. Remember that many dogs react aggressively if confronted with any barrier, such as a cage. If you are interested in a particular animal, ask to take it for a walk on leash, in a controlled area. Remember that even then you may not get an accurate reading on the dog, since it is in a strange environment, with a strange person. If the dog is overly aggressive, or shy, reconsider taking the dog. Try to remain coldly objective. Don't be swayed by appealing eyes, whining, or extreme activity on the part of the animal. Get a second opinion. If you can, take along someone knowledgeable in dogs to help you select.

If you are looking for a female and find an appealing one who has been spayed, chances are good that she came from a situation where the owners felt enough responsibility and concern for the animal to get her spayed. This applies to the neutered male also. Above all, don't go to a shelter on a lark, or because you feel emotionally empty and have an empty pocketbook to match.

CHOOSING A PUPPY FROM A LITTER

As breeders, we have had years of experience in placing puppies. Over the years, we have found that it is not a good idea to allow prospective customers to view a whole litter and pick a puppy on their own. Many times they choose the wrong puppy. All litters have their loners, aggressors, and retreaters. Most people feel that the puppy who immediately breaks out of the litter group and runs up to them, jumping at the fence or barrier, is "the dog for me." We've often heard people say, "I didn't choose him, he chose me — he ran right up to me, and that's how I picked him." Trouble is, often the pup that "runs right up" is the most dominant, and possibly the most prone to behavior problems. Clients who are emotional pushovers and like puppy antics always fall for this approach. Meanwhile, they may ignore other puppies who come up less quickly, or who linger for a while. Yet, one of these might be the right puppy for them.

If you are viewing puppies, try to see each individual puppy alone, in a room. This is the only way to get an idea of the personality of each dog. Don't try to evaluate a puppy in its litter. It's next to impossible. If you are a novice at this kind of selection process, read up on it before visiting the breeder. There are several tests designed to help you select a good puppy suited to your personality and temperament. *Understanding Your Dog* by Dr. Michael Fox and *Behavior Problems in Dogs* by William E. Campbell contain puppy evaluation tests.

Ask the breeder for help in selecting the right puppy. Some breeders will insist on making the choice for you. They might interview you extensively beforehand, to find out what your needs and desires are in a dog. Try to answer their questions honestly and completely. It is an effort for the breeder to do this, and many don't. But if they do interview you about your feelings about a dog, it is a sure sign that they want to place their puppies carefully. The breeder will then match a puppy to you and your situation as closely as possible. If you are new at selecting puppies, or if you are in a deadlock position be-tween two puppies you are consider-ing, trust the breeder to make the right choice. The breeder wants to make a good match and will not try to foist a bad or inferior puppy on you. It is in the breeder's best interest that he make a good match between his clients and his puppies. Most breeders have had previous experience in placing puppies, know how to evaluate puppy behavior, and should be willing to share the results of their observations with you.

6 Researching Canine Roots

Newfoundlands invariably like to swim, retrievers like to retrieve, dachshunds like to dig and burrow, and Siberian huskies love to cavort in the snow. Why? That's what they were bred to do. An amazing number of otherwise educated people do not know the original occupation of their breed of dog. In a time when many people are concerned about their "roots," dog roots go unexplored. Yet knowing the background of your chosen breed can help you to appre-ciate your dog more fully and even aid in solving behavior problems.

Dogs are divided into six basic groups. There are the Sporting breeds, like the spaniels, setters, and retrievers. The Toy group includes smaller dogs like Yorkshire terriers, Chihuahuas, or the papillon. Terriers include the Airedale, schnauzer, and fox terriers. The Working group, for the most part, is comprised of larger dogs like the Newfoundland, the German shepherd dog, and the collie. Hound breeds feature the borzoi, the Afghan, and the droopy-eyed blood-hound. The so-called Non-Sporting dogs include the much-loved Lhasa Apso, the Dalmatian, and the poodle. These categories do not always help to explain the original occupation of the breed. For instance, German shepherd dogs are placed in the Working group, but very few Ger-

Newfoundlands love the water. At a water trial, a Newf tugs a canoe out to a "drowning" victim, rediscovering its canine roots.

original occupation no longer exists is no reason to deprive your dog of its genetic heritage. You can provide some kind of modified activity. For instance, Newfoundlands are rarely called upon to rescue drowning victims anymore (except on the coast of France, where they are still employed), but they might serve as good lifeguards and companions for children on a swimming expedition. A German shepherd living in New Jersey won't have much chance to herd sheep, but it may be of real service as a babysitter and protector. The borzoi, a coursing hound, might no longer have the opportunity to chase down wolves, especially in a country where wolves may end up on the endangered species list in the near future, but it might enjoy the opportunity to gallop freely over a wide open field or golf course. Siberian huskies and other sled dogs were bred selectively to have a strong fore-assembly to pull heavily laden sleds. Is it any wonder that many an urban Siberian husky owner has trouble keeping the dog at a strict heel?

man shepherds work at their original occupation of herding sheep. In fact, the public conception of the breed is so alienated from the dog's original occupation that most people think of the German shepherd automatically as a guard dog, or a police dog. When reminded of the Seeing Eye German shepherd dogs, they begin to scratch the surface of the enormous array of tasks this breed of dog can perform. It's a similar story with many breeds. Sometimes a considerable amount of research is required to find the raison d'être of a given breed.

The objection that your breed's

It's outside the scope of this book to explore the working history of every breed. But it's a good idea to get a book about your particular breed, and if you have a mixed breed, to find out what combination you have and get two or more books if necessary. Some libraries are stocked with books on the better known breeds. The more obscure breeds usually have a national club that is willing to send out pamphlets.

Once you find out the background of your dog, spend some time thinking about how you can reach back and enliven its area of interest. Don't be surprised, however, if you get no reaction from your dog. Many Irish setters are no longer interested in pointing, and some cocker spaniels may have absolutely no interest in a woodcock or even in going into water. In general, breeds that zoom in popularity tend to lose some of their working ability, and their original essence is often diluted as a result of overbreeding and indiscriminate breeding.

On the other hand, searching out your dog's background might give the dog a new lease on life. We once had a Labrador retriever with serious chewing and house-soiling problems. While the dog was with us, we took it into the woods. Immediately, a light went on in the dog's eyes, and when the dog returned from an outing, he was quiet and mellow. Since his master liked to hunt, we suggested having the dog trained in hunting work. Needless to say, the companionship that comes from hunting probably did the dog a world of good, but the chance to express deep-seated instinctual drives might have helped the dog's behavior too. Chewing and house-soiling ceased after the dog became a field dog, and he continued to live in the house.

7 How to Read a Pedigree

Millions of people today are delving into their pasts, researching their family trees. Nowhere is genealogy more currently popular than in the United States. We are intrigued by seemingly unexplainable talents or tendencies, physical traits, drives, or depressions, so we look back to those individuals, living or dead, whom we find melded into the pot of our existence. Though environmental influences play a major role in what we become, they can never increase or decrease what is already within us.

Owning a dog is much like having another member in the family. Here, too, we marvel at all that has gone into the creation of this devoted friend. A mongrel can be a surprise package – a great addition to home life or a mistake that we learn to live with. A purebred gives us a better idea of what's in store for us. Knowing the history of the breed is an invaluable aid in zeroing in on the dog. Knowing the more immediate ancestry is better still.

Many people are curious about

their dog's pedigree but don't know where to begin in breaking the code of numbers and abbreviations. Let's take a sample pedigree. The first page of this pedigree tells us our dog's registered name: New Skete's Nasha von der Lockenheim. We see her A.K.C. registration number and her Call Name: "Natasha."

Most of the information on the first page does not require an explanation. Later on, we will see why Ch. V+Bernd vom Kallengarten, ROM is listed under the words *linebred on*. We will also see why an O.F.A. number is important, but first let's learn about Natasha's parents and grandparents.

Her father, Elko, is a big beautiful, black-and-tan shepherd. He has excellent personality and is intelligent, sensitive, and a bit stubborn at times. He loves to parade around his exercise pen for anyone who will come and watch. He struts about carrying a stick or a ball, throwing out his chest with great pride and nobility — he seems to float effortlessly over the ground. He does not cower or shy but neither is he overly aggressive. Though he is oversized for the show ring, he is a great "people dog."

Elko's father, American and Canadian Champion Hein von der Lockenheim, C.D., ROM, was a first-rate producer. His children have been successful in obedience and conformation, and many have been selected as Seeing Eye dogs. The letters *C.D.* after Hein's name tell us that in the obedience ring he earned the first title in a line of consecutively more difficult tests of intelligence. We will give a brief explanation of these titles toward the end of this chapter. The title *ROM*, or Register of Merit, is earned by German shepherds in America who have produced enough champions to qualify as top producers.

Natasha's mother, Bekky, is a lovely example of a German shepherd bitch. She is medium sized, black and tan with a gentle sloping topline. More sensitive and perhaps more lively than Elko, she is extremely intelligent and very good with children, as is Elko. Her beauty and grace would have won her top honors in the show ring. Graceful too, in her most famous trick: jumping up — all fours — into the arms of her master at his totally unnecessary question, "Do you love me, Bek?"

Here we have absolute trust, complete dedication. Her great nobility of expression — that "almost human" quality — makes Bekky's line, Rigadoon, one of our favorites. In order to preserve this special strain, we must be selective in breeding, knowing that the wrong combination may produce weak ears or missing teeth. We are strongly impressed by Elko's structural soundness, typical of all Hein's progeny as is their zest for life.

Elko carries the genetic factor responsible for producing long-haired German shepherds. Bekky does not have this factor, so there will be no long-haired pups in this litter because both parents must carry the gene. Some of the litter can, however, inherit the gene from Elko and continue passing it on to future offspring.

Elko and Bekky produced a healthy litter of five males and four females.

Elko, the father. Intelligent, sensitive, a bit stubborn at times. Brother Marc poses Elko.

Bekky, the mother. Absolute trust, complete dedication, beauty, grace, femininity.

Natasha is richly pigmented, agile, well structured, and combines the best of her parents' temperaments.

We chose Natasha as the best blend of the two to pass along the traits we admire in their lines.

Natasha has proven to possess a very keen intelligence with a deep desire to please. She has been easily trainable in basic obedience and more advanced retrieving over hurdles. She is very attached to one person, which is true of most shepherds, but she exhibits a certain independence, which is clearly from her father.

We have used Natasha for breeding several times. We are pleased with her litters and she, quite naturally, enjoys being a mother. When bred to a dog with the gene for long coats, no long-haired pups emerged from her litter. This tells us that Natasha did not inherit this gene from her father, because if she did, there should have been at least one pup with long hair.

Our firsthand knowledge of her parents gave us a good idea of what to expect of Natasha. This is something we suggest you ask the breeder of your dog — what are the parents like? Ask for weak points as well as strong ones. You are dealing with a living animal, not some walking perfection. Are the parents energetic or lethargic, stubborn or docile, sensitive or not very sensitive, and to what degree? Try to see both sire and dam in a home setting.

If the father or mother has a tendency to bark, you'll know to be firm in curbing it or to encourage it in their offspring, according to your neighborhood situation. With this background information, you can better appreciate your dog's personality development as you provide the discipline and understanding needed in each individual and unique case.

Getting back to Natasha, her over-all personality is friendly yet protective, and as we can expect from Bekky and Elko, her children are excellent family dogs while some are used for intelligence work, such as tracking drugs for the U.S. Customs. One of her sons, Apollo, works on the Mexican-American border, sniffing out narcotics. Training for this type of work is usually based on the dog's desire to retrieve. Again, genetics are at work: Apollo inherited his mother's fanatic retrieving ability.

Let us look again at Natasha's pedigree. On the second page we find Elko and his parents beginning from the top left-hand corner, and Bekky and her parents beginning from the left-middle of the page. The pedigree shows us the A.K.C. (American Kennel Club) registration numbers beginning with *W* under each name. The A.K.C. divides the breeds into six broad group categories: Sporting, Hound, Working, Terrier, Toy, and Non-Sporting. The first letter of a dog's A.K.C. number reflects the group to which his breed has been assigned. Natasha's breed, German shepherd, is in the Working Group, designated by the initial letter *W* with the A.K.C. numbers.

We note that both Natasha's grandfathers are champions, and Hein, as mentioned before, has earned a C.D. He was also chosen Select Dog at the German Shepherd National Specialty Show. Only a few shepherds are given this honor when competing with other champions from all over America.

Caralon's Elko von der Lockenheim
 	
WB931728
OFA-GS-2322-T
(fulcrum:
    hips & elbows)
	Ch. Caralon's Hein v d
	Lockenheim, C.D.
	
	WA696843
	OFA-GS-112
	American & Canadian
	    Champion
	American Select 1970
	Best-in-Show Dog
	International Work-
	    ing Group Winner
	Top Ten Producer:
	    1972 - 1973
	ROM
		+Bodo vom Katzenkopf
		    SchH I
		    AD

		+Hella v d Spessartheide
		    AD
		    OFA-GS-362

	Chickwood's Gillie
	
	    OFA-GS-800
	    ROM
		Ch.+Bernd vom Kallengarten
		
		    SchH II AD V
		    American Champion
		    ROM

		Ch. Chickwood's Feather
		    American Champion
		    ROM
		    x-rayed normal

New Skete's Bekky of
Rigadoon
 	
WB553760
OFA-GS-4261
	Ch.+Lex von der Vallen-
	darer Höhe
	
	WB27457
	American Champion
	"a" hip certified
	
	A large,large-boned
	male, black saddle &
	muzzle with tan.
		+Munko v d Bimsgrube
		    SchH III FH V
		    "a" hip certified

		+Assie v Steuberturm
		    SchH I V
		    "a" hip certified

	Fortriffe Rigadoon's Rhyme WB71268 OFA-GS-434	Fortriffe Rigadoon's Meteor
		Fortriffe's Liesl of Rigadoon

+Joll aus der Eremitenklause
  SchH III FH AD Kkl-1
  V (75 times V rated)
  Landesgruppen Sieger
	+Arras vom Adam-Riesezwinger
	  SchH III FH V

	+Perle aus der Weingegend SchH I V

+Alma vom Katzenkopf
  SchH I AD Kkl-1
  V
	+Harald vom Haus Tigges
	  SchH III AD Kkl-1 V AmCh 2xAmSelect

	Ellen vom Sieghaus SchH I

+Harald vom Haus Tigges
  SchH III AD Kkl-1 (near ROM)
  American Champion V (31 times)
  Dual American Select
	+Hein vom Richterbach, Interna.Champion
	  SchH III CACIB ROM V, Belgian V-A

	Elwira vom Ekeiplatz SchH III

+Cora von der Spessartheide
  SchH I AD Kkl-1
  V
	+Alex vom Schwanbergsblick
	  SchH I

	+Paula vom Sieghaus SchH I V

+Watzer vom Bad Melle
  SchH III
  V
	+Axel von der Deininghauserheide
	  SchH III DPH FH V-A German Sieger

	+Imme vom Bad Melle SchH II V

+Carin vom Rassweilermühle
  SchH III FH
  V
	+Kuno vom Jungfernsprung
	  SchH III FH V

	+Cora von der Silberweide SchH III FH V

Ch. Llano Estacado's Aquairendal
  American Champion
	Ch. Axel von Poldihaus
	  American Grand Victor Champion ROM

	Waldeslust's Nena
Waldenmark's Zita	Waldenmark's Kip
	Waldenmark's Inga

+Klodo aus der Eremitenklause
  American Champion   ROM
  SchH III German Youth Sieger
	+Arras vom Adam-Riesezwinger
	  SchH III FH V

	+Halla aus der Eremitenklause SchH III FH V-A

+Janka von der Bimsgrube
  SchH II   SG
	+Veus vom Starrenburg
	  SchH III FH V-A German Sieger

	+Gustel von der Bimsgrube SchH I V

+Jörg von der Moselmündung
  SchH III   SG
	+Hein vom Richterbach, Interna. Champion
	  SchH III CACIB ROM V, Belgian V-A

	+Centa von der Pfaffenau SchH III V

+Centi v Pelzgraben
  SchH III FH G
	+Cralo v Segelsberg
	  SchH III FH V

	+Frei v Escherdamm SchH III V

Ch. Mil-Mar's Faro, C.D.
  American Champion
	Red Rock's Gino, C.D.
	  American Grand Victor Champion ROM

	Ch. +Dunja v Wierautal American Champion
Fortriffe's Britta	Nether-Lair's Mighty Max C.D.
	Ch. Fortriffe's Altair American Champion

Ch.+Bernd vom Kallengarten
  SchH II AD V
  American Champion   ROM
	+Watzer vom Bad Melle
	  SchH III V

	+Carin v Rassweilermühle SchH III FH V
Fortriffe's Driad of Rigadoon	Ch. Cato of Fieldstone American Champion
	Ch. Fortriffe's Altair American Champion

We can see that Elko and Bekky as well as their parents have all passed a hip evaluation. When you see an O.F.A. Certification number under a dog's name, it means that the hip X rays have been examined and certified by the Orthopedic Foundation for Animals. Notice that Elko, Bekky, Hein, Gillie, and Rhyme have an O.F.A. number. Natasha, too, has an O.F.A. number on the first page.

Bekky's father, Lex, and his parents are from Germany, where an "a" stamp is given when the dog's hips are approved for breeding. Although much research has been done, the source of crippling hip dysplasia in the larger breeds remains unresolved. We know that heredity plays a major role in this affliction, so we take special care to breed only dogs free of hip dysplasia.

The third, fourth, and fifth generations are for the most part German bloodlines. One name appears both in the third generation on the father's side and in the fourth generation on the mother's side. This is a form of line breeding on Ch. (Champion) V+Bernd vom Kallengarten, ROM, a dog who in a short time has contributed greatly to the breed. His grandson, Ch. Yoncalla's Mike, ROM, is one of a very few dogs ever to be selected twice as Grand Victor Champion at the National Specialty Show.

We notice many of the German-bred dogs have the symbol + before their names; there are many with V ratings, and some with SG ratings. The symbol + tells us that the dog has undergone a strict evaluation at what is known in Germany as the Koerung or Breed Survey. When we find Kk1-1, it means that this dog was placed in a first-class category for breeding use. The V, which is an Excellent rating, and the SG rating, which stands for Very Good, are received at a conformation show in Germany. *Sieger* is a title awarded to the top winner at the annual National Specialty Show corresponding to the American Grand Victor title. Finally, FH stands for a special degree in tracking.

The Schutzhund or Protection Dog title is one you will find on pedigrees of various breeds. There are three titles given, each in order of increasing accomplishment. The examination for each of the three — SchH I, SchH II, and SchH III — has three parts: obedience, protection, and tracking.

Here are the American obedience titles abbreviated:

C.D. — Companion Dog — exercises include: Heel Free, Stand for Examination, Recall, Long Sit, and Long Down.
C.D.X. — Companion Dog Excellent — exercises include: Drop on Recall, Retrieve over High Jump, and Broad Jump.
U.D. — Utility Dog — exercises include: Scent Discrimination, Directed Retrieve, and Directed Jumping.
T.D. — Tracking Dog — exercises include a tracking test.
U.D.T. — Utility Dog Tracker — this dog holds both the U.D. and T.D. titles.

Listed here are only a few of the exercises performed in earning these titles. You can receive a complete list of Obedience Regulations from the American Kennel Club, 51 Madison

Avenue, New York, New York 10010.

Often we find ourselves looking into the eyes of the shepherds we love and seeing more than the individual dog, looking down the corridors of five, ten generations and more, reaching back to an ancestry of planned genetics that has shaped this animal.

We know, too, that dogs are happiest doing what generations of selection have developed in them. Look for determination and stamina in a bloodhound, a soft mouth on the retriever, speed and vision in the basenji, Afghan, and Irish wolfhound. Give your potential pup an aptitude test, but remember: behavior patterns, that is, reaction to external stimuli, are largely inherited. The correct environment and the "T.L.C." are up to you.

8 Where to Find Training

There are several methods of training your dog. You can do it yourself with the aid of books, you can attend obedience school with your dog, or you can send your dog to a training school. By far the most popular method is to do it yourself with or without the aid of books. Chances are, if you are reading this book, you might be interested in training your dog this way. This might be the first, or the tenth, book you have read on dog training in your efforts to get help.

Training manuals can be of great help, and it *is* possible to train your dog alone. For some, the home method is the only possible course, because of financial or geographical considerations. But a better method is to combine reading with another type of training, either public or private.

DOING IT WITH BOOKS

If you *must* train your dog solely with the aid of books, try this method. Get at least three of the training books suggested in the Selected Reading List. For instance, try reading this book and two others, one by a woman trainer and one by a man. All three books will probably cover the same basic exercises, although very few training books cover problem behavior, as this one does. Do not attempt to train your dog with the open book in one hand and the leash in the other. It just doesn't work. Begin by reading one book cover to cover. Then read the second book all the way through. Compare the two methods and reflect on them in the light of what you know about your own dog. The third book can be read while you are actually training, but it's best to read all three before you take out the leash and begin a session with your dog.

This is exactly how we began to train at New Skete. At first we did not have contact with other trainers. Sometimes we found experienced trainers reluctant to part with their techniques. Others were firmly ensconced in certain "schools" of training, faithful disciples of one approach, unable to combine techniques. Since we had no immediate access to obedience clubs, we took each training book with a grain of salt, reading it critically and applying techniques selectively. Meanwhile, our monastery full of dogs served as an indispensable "lab" for perfecting training techniques.

So if you can't get to a training school, or can't leave your dog with a professional to be trained, take heart — you can still train your dog very well with the aid of books. Just be sure to read more than *one* book. Think about the techniques and underlying philosophy in one book, and then go on to another. There are also two excellent periodicals that deal with dog training, listed at the end of this book. It might be good to subscribe to one or both — if only during the period of time you are training your dog. Remember, dog training is an evolving field, and no one author

has all the answers. Read, reflect, react, and *then* begin training.

OBEDIENCE CLASSES

The park obedience school is the second most popular method of training and is an excellent method for many dog owners, especially if they take their dogs at a young age. Try to find a trainer who specializes in "KPT" (Kindergarten Puppy Training) if you have a young dog. Many trainers will ask you to wait to enroll in school until your dog is six, seven, or eight months old. But this might be too late for some dogs, as behavior patterns are set by then. Don't be put off by the "I'm sorry, your dog is just too young" routine. Inquire about KPT training. KPT is a growing movement, and more trainers are becoming interested in working with puppies. As breeders and trainers, we know that training can begin as early as two or three weeks! There are adult brain waves present in the brain of a three-week-old puppy. KPT trainers will be willing to work with your dog the second or third month of its life.

If you have an older dog, by all means enroll in an obedience course. But do so only when you are sure you can attend all the classes. This usually means an eight- to twelve-week commitment. One absence can put your dog behind others in the class, so approach each class seriously and try to be on time, ready for instruction. You must be attentive and alert. Since the instructor will be working with a large number of persons, it might not always be possible to repeat information or answer every question. Try to find a small class of five to ten people if you can. Most classes begin with an introductory session minus the dogs. This session usually prepares the owners for upcoming classes and includes registration and other paperwork, such as vaccination records. You might be asked to sign a waiver concerning any accident that might involve you and your dog. This is a formality, and obedience classes are usually quite safe. During the initial session, some trainers will comment philosophically on their ideas of training. Be sure to take notes, and read and reflect on them at home. The initial class is no less important than the sessions with the dogs, and occasionally it is more important. If a trainer *never* says anything that hints at an underlying philosophy of training, or gives no indication that his or her program has an ethical base, think twice about that particular instructor.

Finding a Good Trainer Finding a good trainer can be a difficult but rewarding search. The first class should give you an idea of what caliber instructor you are dealing with, but by then you might have already plunked down your tuition. Check your area trainers with local training clubs and with friends who have had their dogs trained. Meet the trainer personally before you go to the first class. You may take your dog, but don't ask for an actual evaluation or training session unless you are willing to pay for individual tutoring. Your initial visit should be short. Introduce yourself and your dog. Tell the trainer you are looking forward

to coming to class. Size up the instructor's reaction and level of interest. Be sure to make an appointment before you go. This initial meeting, however brief, should tell you a lot. It might be possible to go to a class the instructor is conducting and watch the progress from the sidelines, minus your dog. Watch how the trainer handles dogs and handlers. Does he or she encourage the handlers? How does he or she touch the dogs? Does he or she stop to answer questions? Are his or her instructions loud, clear, easily understood? Do the dogs and handlers look bored? Does he or she talk too fast?

Beware of instructors who trumpet the number of dogs they have trained, or who try to handle large classes of over twenty dogs alone. A good instructor will have an apprentice or assistant in a large class. If an instructor seems too physical in managing dogs, ask about this. Training methods do include physicality and force, but excesses should never be tolerated. Don't overreact if the instructor applies physical discipline in cases of aggression or extreme disobedience, especially if a handler cannot or will not control a dog. The instructor is responsible for the safety of the handlers and dogs in the class. If you do not understand something the instructor does, *ask about it.*

There are some instances when you should simply quit class and walk out. If an instructor "hangs" a dog, swirls a dog around on the end of a leash, kicks a dog (except to stop a real dog fight), insults a handler, consistently refuses to answer questions, or derides the dogs, quit. But don't jump to conclusions, and ask for clarification before you take action.

Personal Attention Don't expect tons of personal attention in dog obedience school. If you are lucky enough to find an instructor who insists on small classes, you may get a lot of personal help. But in most large classes with a set time limit, the instructor simply can't stop to take five or ten minutes with each person. Remember, you and your dog are a *team* that is working in a *class*. Our clients report that lack of individual attention is the biggest single drawback of park-type obedience courses. Clients needing or desiring much counseling should not expect it in a large class. Some instructors, while quite skilled in teaching basic exercises, have little or no experience in diagnosing more complicated canine behavior, and can sometimes hand out bad remedies.

Flunking Out of Obedience School Don't be discouraged if you "flunk out." You probably won't, but if you do, take it in stride. It certainly does not mean that you or your dog is untrainable. Like many children, some dogs simply cannot take the structured school approach, or they may need individual training. Go to a trainer who will work with your dog alone. Or begin again by a serious study of training manuals, teaching your dog yourself. Ten percent of the dogs we see at New Skete are obedience class dropouts. Almost all respond to a more individual, concentrated approach.

INDIVIDUAL COUNSELING AND TRAINING

Individual training is the third method of training, and is becoming more popular. Leaving your dog with a trainer can often be combined with a long vacation or other absence when you would have to board your dog. Make sure you check the trainer's facilities carefully, ask to see him or her work with an experienced dog, and inquire specifically about what your dog will learn. Many owners wonder about the transfer-of-training problem. "If I leave my dog with another trainer, will he mind me when he gets home?" is a good question. The answer is usually yes — if you follow up on what the trainer does with your dog. Most trainers will give you literature to read while your dog is away. It will pay you to read it.

When you come for your dog, the trainer might have a demonstration for you in a situation where your dog does not know you are there. This can be helpful in two ways. First, it will bring to life the literature you will have read and will let you observe someone else working with your dog, providing an invaluable mirror. Second, since the dog will be anxious to be reunited with you, it will allow the dog to perform without the additional tension of a happy reunion. Most trainers will invite you back for refresher sessions later, if you need them.

Many owners find this method of training a relief and pleasure. Owners who do not have the time or skill to train through books or in a class will find this method a good alternative.

Owners who have flunked out of obedience school, or cannot find an acceptable group instructor, might opt for individual training. Physically handicapped or elderly persons often appreciate individual training, which spares them the bulk of initial highly physical training. Owners who do not have enough time to train their own dogs can choose individual training. Finally, problem dogs are sometimes more responsive to training away from their environments.

All in all, individual training is on a par with class obedience training, and many trainers prefer it to class work. While it is usually more expensive, because of labor and board costs, many owners find it worthwhile.

DOG–OWNER COUNSELING

Deep-seated canine behavior problems, however, cannot be solved simply by attending obedience class. While your dog might become expert with the heel, sit, stay, and lie down commands, the living-room rug might still get chewed, the backyard excavated, or the neighbor's chickens chased and killed. Especially in the case of aggressive behavior, try to get individual attention and dog–owner counseling.

If a good obedience class instructor is hard to find, a good dog–owner counselor is even more elusive. Many owners turn to the local veterinarian. This might be helpful if the veterinarian is skilled in canine behavior and has the time to talk. But many simply cannot take the time to diagnose intricate behavior problems. Some vets keep on file the names of dog trainers

who specialize in dog–owner counseling. You may have to call several area vets before you find one who knows where to find such a counselor. At New Skete we specialize in this kind of training, along with other types of instruction. Dog–owner counseling is a growing, evolving field. It takes time and patience. Not every trainer is interested in it or capable of it. Fortunately, the number of persons who are training themselves in dog–owner counseling is growing. Many veterinarians are becoming interested in problem behavior. Ten years ago, it was nearly impossible to find a professional trainer or veterinarian who would sit down with you and discuss, in detail, why your dog bites, chews, digs, whines, kills other animals, house-soils, or chases cars. Advice on such complicated matters was obtained on the way out the door of the veterinarian's office, or over the coffee table from friends. Ten years from now, individual dog–owner counseling might be the rule, and not the exception.

Remember, too, that trainers are not oracles or gods. They come up against problems that challenge and baffle them. They meet canines they can't understand. Hopefully, they have someone they themselves can turn to for help, as J. Allen Boone did in *Kinship with All Life*. He went to visit Mojave Dan, a wise old desert hermit who lived with a colony of dogs and burros. He asked the hermit to help him understand his dog and get at the truth of the animal. The sage thought for a while and then answered, "There's facts about dogs, and there's opinions about them. The dogs have the facts, and the humans have the opinions. If you want facts about a dog, always get them straight from the dog. If you want opinions, get them from humans."

9 The Concept of Praise in Dog Training

Praise is a misunderstood part of dog training. We asked a number of dog owners what they did to praise their dogs. Here are some sample replies.

Treats. He loves them. Then I pet him all over the head and shoulders.

I give my dog a good rubdown. She rolls over the floor and we have a great time.

You can pet a dog all you want, but nothing matches a good bone.

I talk "baby talk" to my dog, then I pat his head while he's sitting.

My dog nudges me all the time for praise, so I wind up with a hand stroking him ninety-nine percent of the time. We look like a couple going steady.

I never give any praise. Duke comes over and *gets* it! I don't know how many times I've had my cup of coffee spilled in my lap in the morning when he nudges my elbow, or how many times I've been unable to read the evening paper because he's bothering me for attention.

Is praise really necessary? I mean, a good meal, a warm place to sleep, isn't that all they need?

She's only three months old. I know she needs a lot of encouragement and praise, but if I touch her, she breaks down and wets all over the place.

The children play with Yalk all day, but he wants another kind of attention which he gets from me. I don't know how to explain it, but we talk, and it's different from the kids. He'll be outside playing all day, but after dinner, he'll come in very quietly and we have a talk.

Several themes run through these replies: techniques of physical and verbal praise, confusion of food treats with praise, dogs who demand constant praise, owners who do not realize the value of praise, and dogs who are easy or difficult to praise because of behavioral or genetic weaknesses. Surprisingly, we find that many owners consider praise a problem — if they do praise the dog, they feel better and the dog looks happy, and if they don't, they blame themselves for subsequent misbehavior on the part of the dog. What is the proper place of praise?

Let's begin by saying that praise is *absolutely necessary*. It is the cornerstone of any successful dog–owner relationship. It is not a frill, an attached *reward* for "good behavior," but unfortunately, this is the most frequent use of praise. This is part of the misunderstanding of praise — it is used as a bribe to extract good behavior from the dog. But in a healthy dog–owner relationship, praise is virtually an automatic reaction, an *attitude* toward the dog, a way of living with the dog. The most common mistake is to consider praise as simply a *reward*. Rewards do have a place in dog training, but they are not the essence of praise.

PHYSICAL AND VERBAL PRAISE

The concept of praise is two-fold. Praising a dog is a physical and verbal involvement with the animal. It is a delicate matter to combine the two in the right proportions. Each dog needs and desires a different type of praise for different actions. While most owners understand that physical praise means petting their dog, only a few extend any kind of physical contact beyond the head and shoulder regions (see Chapter 22 on massage). Others pound their dogs, and some pet a dog the same way they stroke a cat. Dogs generally like body contact but they do not appreciate slapping motions, heavy pounding, or pulling motions.

Physical praise needs to be measured out according to the situation. We once had a client who was training her dog with us. Each time the dog sank into the "automatic sit," which is a normal part of the heeling process, the client would explode into lavish praise. The dog would heel, dance around, jump up, and generally go berserk. Avoid overloading your dogs with physical praise at the wrong time for the wrong reason. Try to match physical praise to the situation.

One member of our community described how he matches praise to one situation: "Getting up in the morning, my dog stretches, and comes over to the bed just about the time I put my feet on the floor. I vigorously fluff up her mane and ears, ending with stroking and patting her about her muzzle."

Dogs need verbal praise as much as if not more than physical praise. It's difficult to understand what intense verbal praise can mean to a dog until you see it in action. In our early days of dog study, we read about "animation" and the importance of voice tonality in relating with canines. But no book conveyed what we experienced when we heard Helen (Scootie) Sherlock of Caralon Kennels relating with her dogs. She usually has a large number of German shepherd dogs surrounding her, all seeking attention. Scootie is extremely verbal to begin with, and she has a special lingo for her dogs.

Scootie in the midst of morning chores cannot possibly stop to relate physically with each dog. But as she weaves about, feeding, watering, cleaning up the kennel, she manages to *include* each dog. Each one feels personally noticed. They immediately animate and focus their attention on their owner. Since this is their first reaction of the day, they start off with an accepting, willing-to-please attitude toward Scootie that makes the rest of the day easier for everyone.

Notice her technique: she will say a few introductory words, then insert the dog's name. If the dog doesn't realize in advance that it is being addressed, the inclusion of the name makes it a certainty. Remember, it's often difficult to get your dog's attention if you always use the call name first. Try a few happy introductory words.

Ms. Sherlock uses common slang and "CB" radio lingo because she is comfortable with it, and because it delivers strong staccato sounds with clear tone contrasts in short syllables. We've found that many people are verbally inhibited and find it difficult to loosen up and talk to a dog. They find it uncouth, babyish, or demeaning. We've seen some starchy types muffle their embarrassed smiles when they hear us break into a song to one of our dogs, often a personalized jingle about the dog's good or bad qualities. All great trainers *animate* their dogs by talking in happy, peppy tones, employing key affectionate phrases, and using the dog's name frequently. Trainers Wynn Strickland Carson, Jack Godsil, and Don and Joyce Arner make verbal praise a central theme in their training methods, and in their daily life with their dogs. If you feel shy talking to a dog, try role-playing without the dog present. What would you say to the dog if you could carry on a conversation?

TO TREAT OR NOT TO TREAT

Confusion over whether praise is a reward for good behavior or an attitude toward the dog results in the substitution of food treats for physical and verbal praise. Dog-food manufacturers cash in on this confusion by offering dog treats that can be given as rewards, and by playing on the dog owner's insecurities and emotions. The media perpetuate the myth that praise equals reward and that food treats are the best reward; food treats are, therefore, the best way to "praise" your dog.

Treats used in a system of conditioning during formal obedience training can be positive reinforcers — but don't overdo it. The practice is outlawed in the obedience ring. Around the house, on an informal basis, treats should be given only after a "sit" or other command. Dogs that beg, jump on their handlers, steal, get up on counters, or in any way display bad behavior in connection with food should *never* receive treats until the behavior is corrected. Neurotic dogs play games with their owners by nudging them for treats, getting the treat box and dropping it in the owner's lap, and refusing to obey unless treated. Don't tolerate "treat games!" One of our cardinal rules in handling behavioral transgressors is to cut off their supply of treats immediately. While we are not antitreat, treats should always reinforce the dominance of the human in the dog–human relationship. Since the majority of problem-dog situations involve an unhealthy and unbalanced relationship between owner and dog, we suggest suspending treats until the dog's behavior is acceptable and the relationship is balanced.

Another suggestion: instead of commercial dog treats, try an *ice cube*. While some gourmet types will simply let it melt on the floor, many dogs love the crunchiness and coldness of an ice cube. It's a treat that's considerably less expensive than commercial products, and your supply is usually unlimited.

ANTIPRAISE OWNERS

Some owners do not realize the value of praise or may even have a deep-seated prejudice against it. We have an occasional client who declares categorically, "Dogs do not need praise. It spoils them and makes them take advantage of their masters."

One man who felt this way wanted to know if we could train his cocker spaniel to the down in response to a cough. The gentleman explained that he wanted "complete control" over his dog, and that he didn't want to have to bother giving the cocker a command, but thought an "ahem-type" cough should do the trick. He then demonstrated by clearing his throat suggestively. He never praised the dog verbally or physically. "My family had plenty of dogs," he explained, "and none of them needed to be hugged every two seconds." The children in the family sat rigid throughout the interview, contributing little. The wife contradicted the husband at one point and he shot a silencing glance at her, clearing his throat in the same suggestive manner! We explained that dogs need vocal commands and hand signals in order to clearly understand what is asked of them. The cough idea was not possible, especially in a dog–owner relationship that was already faulty, and plagued with chewing and house-soiling problems. Luckily for dogs, this type of autocratic owner is rare.

BEHAVIOR AND GENETIC DIFFICULTIES

Some dogs have behavioral or genetic troubles that make praise difficult. We mentioned earlier the dog that plays the "treat game," cajoling the owner into dishing out tidbits. Some leader-type dogs demand affection and praise constantly, nudging their owners, jumping, yodeling, and making life difficult until they get it. This type of dog always seems to want to be the center of attention. The minute the spotlight shifts elsewhere, as often happens when company arrives or if the owner is on the phone, this dog will begin the "attention game." Visitors will also be nudged and pummeled, sometimes in the genital areas, until they give in and pet the dog. The dog refuses to lie down, and if isolated, does damage. Often the owner has emotionally overloaded the dog by playing the "attention game." The solution should include a program of basic obedience, at least to the come, sit, and stay level, the cessation of all treats, and the reordering of the relationship so that praise is given only in response to an obeyed command like sit, come, or stay.

Genetic faults often complicate praise-giving. Submissive urination in puppies and occasionally in older dogs often happens in response to *physical* praise. Ignore this type of wetting, and try to use *verbal* praise rather than physical praise until the dog develops more bladder control. Do not discipline submissive urination. It is not the same as house-soiling.

Other dogs come from bloodlines that are so hyperactive that praise

elicits excessive shaking and nervousness. Again, try to develop verbal praise with this type of dog. Some dogs practically have a nervous breakdown when physically praised. Enthusiastic high-intensity verbal praise usually does not elicit the same response. Physical praise for nervous dogs should be given only when the dog has responded to the sit command and is anchored. Jumping up can then be controlled.

Praise, then, is more than treats, more than an occasional physical pat, and more than a reward for good actions. Praise is an *attitude*, a *stance*. Dogs who live in an atmosphere of praise come to love the human voice. They are more trusting and accepting. They are approachable by strangers but not demanding. Dogs confident of praise from their owners do not live on the edge of an emotional abyss, always seeking out attention, and sulking when they do not get it. If praise is part of your *attitude* toward your dog, you have a rich and exciting relationship ahead.

10 **Discipline: The Taboo Topic**

Some dog-training books never mention discipline for bad behavior.

Yet, in our consultations with dog owners, questions about it are frequent. Owners run a gamut of emotions and responses in their attitudes toward correcting their dogs. Here are some sample quotes we've collected over the years, when we asked the question "Do you discipline your dog for bad behavior, and if so, how?"

I hit him on the rump with a rolled-up newspaper. Sometimes I have to chase him. He knows when he's done wrong.

I yell and say, "No, no," and she slinks and hangs her head. But then she messes in the same place the very next day.

When I disciplined the dog, the children would scream and cry, so I gave up. I didn't want the kids to think I was hurting the dog.

Even if I raise my hand to smack Queenie, she bares her teeth. It's like living with Hitler.

I never hit my children, and I never hit my dog.

One dog we had — we beat on him pretty hard. We broke his spirit and he took off on us. I don't want that to happen again.

We discipline by hitting the dog over the head with a stick. It works.

From puppyhood on, I punished my dog by smacking her rear end. Then, I went to obedience school when she was about eight months old. The instructor said to give the dog a light tap on the rear end to get her to sit. This didn't work with my dog. She would urinate when I touched her rear end. She thought she was being punished. I had to find another method of teaching the sit, and I fell behind in the class.

I simply don't believe in discipline, physical or otherwise. Yes, I am my dog's maid. I don't like the arrangement but I've seen other dogs who were hit, and they always look sad.

My dog cheats, steals, craps in the house, and has bitten three people. You tell me to discipline him. Okay, where do I start?

If I even look at Buffy cross-eyed, that's enough discipline for her.

I lost control one day and smacked Butch under the chin for stealing a rib roast. He hasn't stolen anything for three months. I think I got through to him.

On the rear end, with a hair brush.

A good kick usually does the trick.

For housebreaking, I rub his nose in it, and for chewing, I cram it down his throat.

There's a great deal of inconsistency in my family. Some are pacifists who would sooner die than hit the dog. Others are bullies and would torture the thing if they got the chance.

A good night outside usually shapes them up. Out into the cold!

Let me warn you: if a trainer ever hit my dog, I'd kill him.

I say no, King looks away, and then I end it. I can't do anything else once I look at his face.

I want to understand when and how to discipline my dog, but the training books talk about everything but that, and I feel I might do something wrong. What exactly do you do?

For the life of me, I don't know why Prince won't stop chewing. I beat him every night!

Perhaps one reason dog discipline is shrouded in mystery is that people are afraid of the whole subject. Let's face it: no one likes to hit a dog. Another aspect that influences owners is the periodic flurry of horror stories about dog-beaters, irresponsible trainers, and general inhumane treatment of dogs. Simple and effective discipline for disobedience and bad behavior then gets confused with inhumane treatment. One dog owner reported that an eccentric animal-rights worker, or "humaniac" as our client called her, threatened to call the Humane Society when she saw the client smack her dog for chasing another dog. There will always be extreme responses.

In our experience, here are the situations we feel may merit both physical and verbal discipline:

Aggression with humans — defined in a social context as excessive barking, growling, charging, chasing, nipping, or biting a human.
House-soiling — defecation or urination in the house or in any other improper place.
Stealing — theft of food, or objects.
Persistent destructive behavior — destructive chewing, digging, or house-wrecking not the result of puppy antics or accidents.
Aggression with other dogs — defined as in-species fighting, usually between two males, but possible between a male and a female or two females.

We repeat, these situations may merit physical discipline. Since no book can pretend to analyze every individual dog and owner situation, we feel obligated to emphasize from the outset that discipline is never an arbitrary training technique to be applied to each and every dog for all offenses. We do, however, believe that physical and verbal discipline can be an effective technique. The best policy if you experience any of the above problems is to consult a qualified trainer or veterinarian for evaluation of your individual situation (see Chapter 8, "Where to Find Training").

If discipline is decided upon as a training technique, it should be the proper kind of discipline. We feel we have developed several methods that depend less on violent physical force than on timing, a flair for drama, and the element of surprise. We feel an obligation, as responsible trainers, to map out these methods, rather than simply skip the topic because it is unpleasant. Dog owners want to know what to do.

Many owners use an object when disciplining their dogs. The overwhelming choice seems to be the rolled-up newspaper. We feel that discipline should be administered with the owner's hand. The hand that feeds is the hand that punishes. Do not use objects of any kind to discipline your dog.

*The wrong way to discipline a dog.
Never use an object. Never discipline
from above or behind.*

*One way of disciplining is to sit the dog
and use upward strokes under the chin.*

PHYSICAL DISCIPLINE UNDER THE CHIN

One way of disciplining the dog is under its chin. The dog should be anchored in the sitting position. Your fingers meet the underside of the dog's mouth in an upward motion. It is essential first to sit the dog, by pulling up on the training collar or pushing down on the animal's rear end. This also rivets the dog's attention upward toward the owner's eyes, so that eye contact can be made. Eye contact is very important in discipline. Wolves disciplining each other make eye contact. Never hit a dog from above. Your fingers should be closed together, your palm flat.

How hard do you hit the dog? A good general rule is that if you did not get a response, a yelp or other sign, after the first hit, it wasn't hard enough. Remember, one good correction will save you fifty. You cannot hurt the dog with this method, or cause irreparable damage. Your contact must be firm.

Keep one hand on the training collar, and tighten it, so that the dog remains sitting. Insert your index finger into the ring of the training collar, and wrap your fingers around the extension you will have when it is pulled snugly. Keep this tension on as you discipline the dog with the other hand. Keep the dog sitting.

THE SHAKEDOWN

An alternative means of discipline, often just as effective as the under-the-chin method, is the shakedown. This method is suggested for shy dogs and for dogs who have large jowls (St. Bernards, Newfoundlands, some boxers), for whom chin discipline would not be as effective. We also suggest this alternative method for puppies, until they are at least six months old. We repeat: physical discipline should be reserved for the heinous canine crimes mentioned earlier, not meted out for every episode of bad behavior. Verbal correction might suffice for many dogs, but you should know more than one method of discipline before the unfortunate necessity of using one arises.

In the shakedown the dog is sitting, anchored in place with tension on the training collar. When you have seated the dog, and are sure it will not move, wheel around in front of it and kneel down. Grasp the scruff of the dog's neck with both hands and lift it right off its front feet into the air. Look directly into the dog's face, and shake the dog back and forth in quick, firm motions, gradually lowering the dog. Scold the dog while you look at it, and keep it elevated a good thirty seconds. It may be difficult to raise some larger breeds, in which case you will have to sacrifice this part of the procedure. Most dogs, however, can be lifted up off their front feet with a little effort.

After discipline in this fashion, the dog will be shaken up mentally and physically. As in the previous method, eye contact is essential. This method is also suggested for dogs that respond aggressively to under-the-chin correction, since it is more difficult to retaliate in the shakedown position. When you grasp the dog under its chin,

The shakedown. Kneel, grasp both sides of the dog's neck fur, and elevate the dog.
Make eye contact and shake back and forth as you scold.

make sure that you have one or both thumbs looped under the training collar, to stop the dog from breaking away. With your fingers, grab hold of quite a bit of neck scruff, and hold it firmly.

For young puppies amend this method somewhat. First, cut down on the intensity and duration of your correction. A young pup should be disciplined by simply grabbing with one hand the scruff of the neck and giving it a good shake. This method approximates the technique a mother of a litter uses to keep order in the litter, to stop fighting between litter members, or to help wean her pups away from her to solid food. Discipline methods that reflect instinctual canine behavior will communicate displeasure in ways a dog can understand. Other corrections like throwing or hitting the dog with objects, spanking with newspapers, or simple pleading only serve human, not canine, ends, and do not communicate displeasure clearly to the dog.

THE ALPHA-WOLF ROLL-OVER

This disciplinary technique is nicknamed for the type of punishment the lead wolf dishes out to misbehaving members of the pack. We couple it with the regular discipline procedures described earlier. After you have anchored and disciplined the dog for deliberate disobedience or for one of the "big offenses" that merit physical discipline, add the Alpha-wolf roll-over. Use the Alpha-wolf roll-over especially in cases of aggression, chronic chasing of people or objects,

fighting with other dogs, or predation.

Immediately after phase one of the discipline procedure, which is anchoring (sitting) the dog and disciplining it under the chin or with the shakedown, place the dog on a down. If the dog does not know the down, use one of the techniques described in detail in the obedience section to get the dog down immediately. Be very abrupt and curt about this. Firmly grasp the scruff of the dog's neck with one hand, as you crouch over the dog on one knee. Balance yourself with the other hand and keep it ready to correct any biting attempts. If you have properly disciplined your dog with the anchored sitting or shakedown methods, it will not be too anxious to cause you further trouble at this point. Grasping the scruff of the dog's neck firmly, roll the dog over onto its back. When you roll the dog over, make your movement quick, firm, to the point. Don't casually guide the dog over as if you were going to groom it or play with it. Shove the dog onto its back with vigor. At this point, most dogs will go into the classic submissive posture of all canids. The dog will bend its front paws to its chest, spread its legs wide open, push back its ears, possibly tuck its tail between its legs, and look up fearfully. This is the moment to make eye contact, and continue scolding the dog. Keep the dog pinned on its back by applying steady pressure with your hand on its neck area. Your verbal discipline may now be quieter, but no less firm and direct than it was during the first phase of discipline. You are acting as the Alpha-wolf. In a

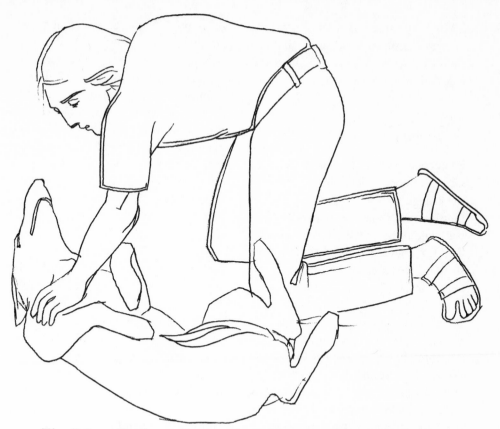

The Alpha-wolf roll-over. Drama and surprise are essential in this technique.

wolf pack the leader will often pin subordinates for misbehavior in this same position. While the Alpha-wolf rarely causes the subordinate any physical harm, the point is clearly made. Often the subordinate wolf will hold this submissive position for a few moments while the Alpha-wolf raises his head and looks down into the eyes of the pinned wolf. This and other methods of dominance and correction are means of keeping order in the wolf pack without overt physical harm. On the domestic scene, you can use this instinctual correction to "seal" your disciplinary techniques. Let us note that many dogs may never

need such physical discipline. But if you have a dog that does, it seems better to administer discipline effectively and meaningfully once, rather than dozens of times in an ineffective way.

The disciplinary techniques explained in this section should not be applied haphazardly and for slight misbehavior. There is always the chance that autocratic dog owners, having learned discipline techniques, will misuse them. But owners who are physically or verbally domineering wind up with cringing, neurotic dogs. Discipline, like praise, must be meaningful. It must communicate the owner's displeasure clearly, and on the dog's level of understanding and perception.

THE VERBAL ELEMENT IN DISCIPLINE

Some dog owners find it difficult to say anything when they discipline their dogs, as they are intent on the physical manipulation required. Verbal scolding is essential. It requires a flair for drama and good timing. The standard vocabulary for canine misbehavior is "No, no," and "Shame, shame," and perhaps "Bad dog!" Most of us have a whole speech prepared inside, ready to spill out, whenever we come upon or witness the results of our dog's misbehavior. We refrain from saying anything more than these pat phrases. Why?

One client put it this way: "Loddie does something wrong, and I know exactly what I want to say. I even know the tone of voice I want to use. But something tightens up inside of me." Another client said, "If I yell at the dog, the children think I am hurting it." Another dog owner reflected, "I've always been taught control over my temper. If you get mad, control it. Keep it all in. Although I *am* having tremendous problems with this dog, I can't see myself disciplining it physically or verbally. I just can't stand the feelings I get inside myself when I get angry."

The first thing we try to explain is that discipline need not be a terrible ordeal, and that anger has a natural place in life. Dog discipline, if approached correctly and with a sense of humor, is more play-acting than anything else, although the dog must not know it. On the other hand, the element of force is involved. But all training methods use force to some degree. In discipline, the owner puts the dog in a subordinate position and plays the Alpha-wolf in much the same way the leader of a wolf pack does. We encourage drama, timing, and surprise by having clients role-play situations when they might need to discipline their dogs. If an owner can successfully role-play finding a mess in the middle of the living room rug ten minutes before a dinner party, or having a fight break out between his or her dog and the neighborhood rival, or any number of other catastrophic canine capers, then the actual occurrence of such events can be approached more easily. So if you feel ill at ease with discipline, get a large pillow and pretend.

The tone of your voice is important and should be very sharp, loud, and commanding. Some dog owners are naturally verbally dominant, some are not, but a happy medium can be approached by all. Learn to say "no," not in a whining, pleading tone, but as if you were throwing a verbal rock at the dog. If need be, go into a closet and practice belting out "no!"

DOGS ARE NOT CHILDREN

One woman came to us with a Pekingese with persistent chewing problems. She approached all dog problems as she would child problems. She quoted specialists who take the permissive approach to child-raising. Some information on the dog's quite different background helped her to see the differences between her Pekingese and a child. Obviously, there are some analogies between a dog and a child that can be drawn, but discipline is not one of them. Puppies in litters often discipline each other, jostling, shoving, and pinning each other. The mother of the litter disciplines the litter members with gentle bites. It should be remembered that dogs mature much faster than humans, and their receptivity to discipline is in a different sphere from ours. Don't be afraid to discipline your dog, but do it correctly and on a level that the dog can understand.

REVIEW THESE DISCIPLINE DO'S AND DON'T'S

1. Go and get the dog. Never call a dog to you and then discipline it. Even if a chase is involved, go and get the dog.
2. Sit the dog. Put tension on the training collar by inserting your index finger in one ring, and pulling it snug. If the dog doesn't sit, press down on its rear. Don't begin disciplining until the dog is sitting and anchored. Otherwise, the dog can more easily scoot away from you and avoid correction.
3. Make eye contact with the dog.
4. Discipline with the under-the-chin or shakedown methods as described.
5. Never use an object to discipline.
6. Never hit from above.
7. Remember to be dramatic.
8. Remain passive for one-half hour after disciplining.

MAKING UP AFTER DISCIPLINE

Just as it is important to administer meaningful discipline quickly and firmly when your dog commits a big offense, it is also essential to "make up" later. This "making up" process does not have to be emotionally wrenching or cathartic. After you discipline your dog, you should remain passive for at least half an hour, not speaking to the dog and avoiding eye contact. If you do attempt to make eye contact with your dog at this time, chances are your dog will avoid looking at you. Your dog will want to make contact with you, but in its own time. Your dog will behave after discipline very much as a wolf does. Your dog may look away, gaze down at the floor, or look like it is trying to melt into the wall. This is a natural reaction of submission that should not be interfered with by the distraught owner. Unfortunately, when the dog displays these reactions after discipline, many owners go to the dog and coddle it, trying to "cheer it up." When they approach, they may find that the animal remains motionless or trembles. This makes the owner feel even more guilty.

The fact is, the animal simply needs a certain amount of time to readjust. Just leave the dog alone for a half hour. On the other hand, if the dog shows no signs of submission or deference after discipline, you should reexamine how firm you were in disciplining. If your dog comes up to you and nudges you for attention five minutes after you have disciplined it, chances are the dog didn't get the point.

After a half hour, do something friendly with your dog. Take a walk or a car ride, give the dog its favorite toy, or speak softly and encouragingly to the dog. Avoid dramatic make-up gestures, like food treats or robust play sessions. Some dogs may need more building up than others, and you will have to size up your own dog. The important point is to be big enough to make up, but not so guilt-ridden and overbearing that you fail to give the dog the readjusting time it naturally needs after an effective correction.

In mapping out these techniques for discipline and making up afterward, we realize that domineering owners can easily abuse them. Although there is a tendency for new dog owners to be easy with their pets, others who are oblivious to how deeply sensitive a dog is, and how deeply sensitive they must be in return, will resort to physical discipline when a sharp reprimand or eye contact would be enough. Dogs who slink and cower are sometimes the wards of such autocrats. We feel, however, that it is important to mention discipline procedures and explain them, since dog owners may occasionally need them, and effective and controlled use of them will help your overall rapport and increase your enjoyment of your dog.

11 What's Cooking?

A sound mind in a sound body! Before we can go on to work on improving our pet's behavior, it is paramount that he be physically healthy. Really healthy, not just looking okay. Dogs can go on functioning well to all appearances while in fact they are in serious, poor condition. In time, just as with us, dogs, too, will begin to break down in their behavior, and many an owner will stand there concerned and baffled as to what has caused this change. The answer lies in the food dish.

In supplying our dog with a diet that will maintain its condition at its best, we need a realistic view of the whole picture. Avoid falling into sloppy habits that can only hurt your dog in the final analysis. Feed the dog what it needs, not what you think it needs!

Dry kibble should be the basic dog food. Many dry foods are soybean based, but some of the better brands (Iams, Science Diet) are made from meat meal and may be available only through special distributors. These higher-priced, more sophisticated feeds are worth looking into. Any kibble you feed should contain at least twenty-two percent protein, preferably more. Dry-food companies that conduct research farms where nutritional experiments are conducted to back up the claims on the back of the package are usually good bets.

Canine nutrition is a subject of much discussion, but in general we have had success with our dogs using the finer kibbles and supplements. The reputable feed producer has usually included proper dosages of vitamins and other necessary ingredients in the preparation of the kibble, but often a diet of kibble alone can be deficient. We suggest supplementing the kibble with raw meat, preferably tripe or meat fresh frozen specifically for dogs. Canned meats and scraps from your own table, while more readily available and convenient, do not compare with specially prepared raw meat. Here's one instance when you are feeding the dog what it likes!

Meat should not constitute more than twenty-five percent of the dog's diet. The American tendency is to go overboard on meat. Raw meat, frozen meat, tripe, canned meat or table scraps — none should exceed more than one cup at each meal.

Two smaller meals are healthier than one large meal. A smaller portion is usually more easily digested. The risk of torsion (stomach bloat) in many breeds is serious and often fatal, and smaller portions help to avoid this problem. Two feedings help prevent hunger tension that can be a factor in problem behavior like chew-ing, and can help cut down begging behavior between meals.

Puppies from the time of weaning to four months of age require three meals a day. The pup is growing in leaps and bounds, and its stomach cannot take an overload of food all at once. The feeding times need to be adhered to strictly, and should be basically in the morning, at noon, and in the early evening. The evening repast should be no later than five or six o'clock, to give the puppy time to eliminate before retiring. Puppies generally need twice the number of calories and general nourishment of older dogs. They benefit by twice-a-week supplements of yoghurt, which helps to restore intestinal flora, and wheat germ, which is rich in B vitamins and eggs.

A supply of fresh water is a must. Every adult dog should have access to cool, clean water at frequent intervals. Puppies can tend to gulp too much water, and should be offered water periodically, rather than have free access to it. This is especially true during house-training. If a pup or older dog spends time outdoors in the sun, it should have all the water it needs. Water should be taken up at night, especially if you are house-training a young puppy.

Never, never refuse to feed your dog as a punishment. Behavior and health are related, but not to the degree that withholding food will accomplish any positive good in behavior. The feeding time should be marked by affection and praise. Since the dog's need for health is paramount, good or bad behavior should not have anything to do with regular meals. This may seem like simple common sense, but we have talked with some dog owners who try to prod their pets into good behavior by cutting off their basic rations.

TREATS

Treats fall into two categories. First, many people award their pooches for doing well in training exercises. This practice is fine until your dog starts begging or you run out of treats. Training sessions are better accompanied by verbal and physical praise and only rarely a tasty morsel.*

An occasional treat for your dog is not out of order and does serve to cement your mutual relationship. It's a good idea to ask the dog to sit before treating it. This only takes a second and can help the dog learn the command. We strongly advise against treats at the table. During meals, your pet should lie near your feet or elsewhere in the dining room. Do not banish your dog from the room at this time. Teach the dog the down and down-stay so he can be included in the experience, but not at the table. It is not a "torture" for the dog to watch its owners eat — it is a pleasure to be included. Never let the pet sit at the table. Treats after dinner for a successful down-stay are fine, but whenever you treat the dog, indicate clearly when the treat-time is over. Tell the pet kindly but firmly that there is no more and to take its place.

Dogs, like people, can be fussy eaters. This can frustrate you since you will naturally be concerned about the causes and implications of such fussiness. Don't lose your temper. Anger and pleading will not solve anything. The best approach is simply to set the dish before your dog for a few minutes and leave the dog alone. If there is no reaction, take the food up and reoffer it later. Do not try to coax the dog to eat. In extreme cases, hand feeding might work if you must get a few mouthfuls into your pet. But don't do this frequently or your pet will come to rely on it. Something might be askew about your dog's health when it does not eat, and other times a change in the weather or the addition of meat to the food might perk up the appetite. If such behavior persists, and is not characteristic of your dog, see your vet.

How much should your dog eat? Begin by taking a good look at your friend. Is your dog lean or too fat? Don't rely completely on the statistics on the back of dog-food packages to gauge how much your pet should be eating. These set tables do not take into account the peculiar traits of many dogs, their high or low energy levels, the amount of exercise they receive, or their ability to metabolize certain types of food. Try to keep your dog on the lean side. Extra weight means extra work for the dog who has to haul around those pounds. In pups, leanness and a pronounced stomach could mean worms, so it is wise to have a stool sample analyzed at your vet every three months until the dog is one year old, and every six months after that. The *Gaines Guide to Canine Nutrition* (Gaines Research Center, White Plains, New York

* Dr. Benjamin Hart, "Canine Behavior: Problems with Feeding Behavior," *Canine Practice* (August 1976), pp. 10–14.

10625) contains a good feeding chart for dogs of various ages and sizes. More books on canine nutrition are recommended in the reading list.

Overweight dogs usually suffer from too much food and too little exercise. Spaying a female or neutering a male should not increase the animal's weight, if the diet is properly controlled. In large breeds where hip dysplasia is a frequent condition, overweight can cause suffering and can further the progression of their dysplastic condition.

Commercial feeds may not do enough to help your dog's coat stay in top condition. Fats are required in the diet for good coat sheen. Try an egg or three teaspoons of corn oil a day until the coat improves. Raw ground beef, cottage cheese, and cooked eggs can aid muscle tone. Cooking beef liver and hamburger destroys much of the vitamin content. Feed meat (except for pork) raw. Freeze meat at zero degrees Fahrenheit before thawing and feeding. Freezing will destroy any possible harmful bacteria. Liver should not be fed every day, as it can induce diarrhea. A quarter of a cup of liver every other day is sufficient. Always cook pork.

Coprophagia, or stool eating, may indicate a deficiency in diet or may be an obnoxious bad habit. If your dog has this habit, which is not uncommon, you will need to supervise the dog's defecation times, and immediately after the dog has finished eliminating, call it in. Pick up after your dog, especially if he has later access to the stools. Dogs confined to exercise pens and unsupervised may be reacting to boredom or a lack of play toys. There may be the possibility that an enzyme is lacking in the dog's system and the dog is attempting to make up for the deficiency by stool-eating. Try sprinkling his food with Accent. This addition seems to make the stool unattractive and may make up for the missing enzyme. Concoctions of Tabasco sauce and vinegar on the stools to deter your dog from munching might help.

PROBLEM BEHAVIOR AND NUTRITION

If you are experiencing behavior problems with your dog dietary changes might be beneficial. William E. Campbell, in his nutritional studies involving problem dogs, has found that the general approach of feeding higher protein and lowering the carbohydrate intake has been effective in two ways.* First, conditioning to commands and signals seems to be better retained. Second, dogs appear less hyperactive and less disturbed by external stimuli, like passing cars, other dogs barking, and loud noises. He suggests the supplement of a B complex vitamin formula to the diet to take care of any possible thiamin or niacin deficiencies that may be connected with poorly conditioned reflex formation and hyperactivity. He wisely calls the addition of B complex good "behavioral insurance." Our work with problem dogs bears out these findings. It seems difficult to find a B complex vitamin formulated for dogs, so we usually suggest human

* William E. Campbell, *Behavior Problems in Dogs* (American Vet. Publications, 1975), chapter 5: "Nutrition and Problem Behavior."

vitamins. We always emphasize that this is not "drug therapy" but simply the addition of a vitamin. Clients who use vitamins as a family and follow healthy eating habits themselves readily grasp our rationale, while families with poor nutritional habits often feed their dogs poorly, too.

In cases of problem behavior we usually suggest cutting off the problem dog's supply of treats and suspending any "junk" foods that contain red dyes or high amounts of sugar. We suggest two feedings a day to prevent hunger tension. Finally, we teach clients how to decipher dog-food labels and the advertising psychology used by pet-food companies.

When you consult a veterinarian about nutritional problems or ask for advice, make sure you have written down exactly what you have fed your dog recently, no matter what it is. Don't expect a vet to provide you with helpful information unless he or she knows what you have been feeding your dog previously, what you can afford, and a basic health history of your dog.

Environments

12 Canine Environments

There are four basic types of canine environments: the city, the suburbs, the country, and the life of the outdoor dog. Each presents a different life-style to the dog and each holds the potential for fostering its own set of problems. Contrary to popular belief, there is no ideal setting for each and every dog. The myth that no dog can live happily in a large city is being debunked daily as thousands of dogs manage to exist with smog, skyscrapers, noise, pollution, and lack of space. The reverse myth that a dog can find true happiness on a farm certainly doesn't apply to all dogs, since country dogs are presented with a set of problems all their own.

While we do not pretend to point out every pitfall in each particular setting, we do attempt to pinpoint some of the main problems peculiar to each locale. Some dogs will spend part of their lives in all four settings, and others might move dramatically between city and country, even in the course of a year. No matter what the locale, the smart dog owner avoids the temptation to blame the locale for his dog's problems and behavioral quirks. While different environments might trigger idiosyncrasies, training can usually help your dog overcome them.

Don't be afraid to have a dog simply on the basis of where you live. Dogs can be happy almost anywhere, if their lives are properly structured, and if they are conditioned to the particular environment and its demands. Finally, the owner must reflect on his canine's environment, and try to make it as healthy as possible. These chapters will help you to do that.

13 City Life

Is it impossible to own a dog in a large American city? Apparently, the answer is no, as thousands do just that. They own dogs of all sizes and breeds, not just the typical apartment dogs. As the crime rate increases in some cities, many purchase large dogs with a "protection image." German shepherd dogs and Doberman pinschers are becoming more popular in urban areas, and poodles and other smaller breeds have been living there for years. It is possible to have a happy dog in a large city, but it takes time, dedication, and money.

One of the most obvious problems is providing your dog with a balanced amount of exercise every day. If you are in the city and own a dog, you will need to commit yourself to an exercise program of one, and preferably two, exercise outings each day. The length of the walk will depend on the breed you own. These walks should entail more than simply time outdoors for the dog to eliminate. They must be exercise outings in which the dog is walked at length or allowed to run. The walk will most probably have to be on leash, since almost all cities have strict leash laws. Your dog will need to go out every day, fair weather or foul, summer and winter. If you live in an upper-floor apartment there may be no convenient way to let your dog out for defecating and expect it to return to your apartment. This will mean the animal's access to the outdoors depends on someone. There can be no avoiding the responsibility of taking the pet out.

The exercise problem is one of the most obvious drawbacks to keeping a dog in the city, and yet, it's not as bad as all that. No matter where a dog lives, it needs the same amount of exercise and it needs to go out to eliminate. The major difference in the city is that these activities must be regulated on leash, for the most part. This means you must accompany your dog. Many people find it helpful to set up a daily schedule fitting in some kind of exercise for themselves along with their dog. In New York, for instance, joggers hold their dogs on leash as both run around in parks. In some large cities, groups of dog owners have cooperated in installing large pens where dogs can be brought for exercise, play, and elimination purposes, while the owners read or chat. For those with large or extremely active breeds, a program of roadwork (see Chapter 24, "One for the Road") provides the dog with exercise even if the owner cannot walk along. But roadwork may be difficult in the city unless you live near a large park where traffic is minimal.

If you own a city dog, one of the most important skills you can teach it is to fetch. Ten minutes of fetching can provide a hearty exercise session for most dogs and it will utilize many more muscles than mere walking. A fetch session should be on the daily agenda of every city dog. Frisbees, sticks, or a deflated football are objects that can be located more easily than a regular ball after a throw. Every big city park must be strewn with assorted size balls intended to be retrieved by dogs but eventually thrown too far and lost. Just as young people discovered the Frisbee in the sixties, dogs seem to be enjoying it now.

"I wouldn't own a dog in the city — it would never get any fresh air!" This common complaint has some merit. Air pollution in some cities is unremitting and the air inside is usually cleaner than the air outside. Take the normal precautions for your dog that you would take for yourself. Don't expose the dog to noxious vehicular exhaust if you can help it. Try to get your dog out onto grass at least once a day, even if it is only a small patch of greenery. Don't blow cigarette smoke in your dog's face, even in jest.

Noise pollution is actually more of a problem to dogs than air pollution. Honking horns, sirens, airplanes, sonic booms, and crowd noises all take their toll on the city dog. Again, use the same precautions for your dog you would take for yourself. Avoid walking past construction projects if you can avoid it, because loud sudden machinery noises can make even the best-trained dog break heel and dart away. Narrow, thin alleys, or precarious, temporary construction crossings can be a problem. Remember, not all dogs are of the caliber of Seeing Eye dogs, which are able to cope with city stress because they are genetically and educationally prepared. When you must traverse an area where noise is deafening, hold the dog near to you on leash, and cup one hand around the dog's neck until the noise dies down or you pass out of its range. This comforting body contact can help the dog cope with the noise more easily. Dogs should not be allowed to run free in city parks unless they are completely controllable. In some cities the law may forbid off-lead dogs altogether. Even city parks can be a stress for the dog and can provoke strange behavioral reactions. For instance, never allow the dog to run free with strange children. Don't allow noisy children to crowd around your dog. Groups of screaming children have often triggered biting incidents or encouraged playful dogs to jump up. A child who is jumped on in play, and then falls and screams, can

be perceived as prey by a dog, with occasionally tragic results.

The city dog needs to be able to deal with an incredible array of strangers each day. Many humans in cities simply go on "automatic pilot" and pass strangers without seeing particular faces. This ability to screen out distractions is more difficult for dogs to acquire. The dog remains interested, in a positive or negative way, in practically every human and dog it passes. Pedestrians may react in a variety of ways, from fear, to over-effusive affection, to outright disdain or hostility. There is simply no way to predict the variety of reactions, so the best approach is to expose your dog to all possibilities in a structured training session. Accustom your dog to being approached, petted, and also possibly rebuffed.

A leadership role by the master, and heeling practice, can help rivet the dog to its owner, but remember that heeling is always more difficult in the city. There are simply more distractions, more opportunities to lag behind and investigate or to lunge ahead. If you follow the heeling methods described in this book and are sure to train your dog to heel by using distractions in your training sessions (traffic, other dogs, working in crowds), your dog should be controllable and able to meet any situation on the street.

In an elevator, you and your dog might be squeezed in with a crowd of other people. Accustom your dog to riding in an empty one first, before attempting to ride in a full elevator. If your dog is either prone to aggressive reactions, or simply wilts if caught in a crush of people, you will have to be wary of elevators, crowded hallways, and rush-hour crowds on city streets. If this is a problem for you, keep your dog on leash, and its training collar high around its neck for more control. Gradual exposure to these situations often improves a dog's performance.

No need to mention the foolishness of allowing a dog to run free in an urban area. A dog's chances of survival are slim. A free-roving city dog can galavant around continually, chased by dog catchers and others. Life for this dog soon becomes the equivalent of guerrilla warfare, a daily ritual of scavenging, fighting, and avoiding capture. Studies have been done on the behavior of free-roving urban dogs and they show that these dogs learn to move quickly.* They can be so cunning that they avoid capture for weeks. If you live in a congested area and let your dog run free unsupervised it may be recruited into one of these canine gangs. The end that awaits these vagabonds is the pound and probable euthanasia.

Since city dogs are so restricted, they often wind up just staying at home alone. It's just not possible to take the dog everywhere in the city. Even if the dog can stay in the car comfortably, in some cities there is a very real chance that the dog could be stolen. On the other hand, most city

* See Alan M. Beck, "The Ecology of 'Feral' and Free-Roving Dogs in Baltimore," in *The Wild Canids, Their Systematics, Behavioral Ecology and Evolution,* ed. Michael W. Fox (New York: Van Nostrand Reinhold, 1975). Mr. Beck estimates that "there is one free-roving dog for every nine humans in Baltimore."

pets serve a need for protection and security, so they are left behind to guard the owner's belongings. The resulting isolation, accompanied by a backdrop of urban noise, is often a prelude to incessant barking, destructive chewing, or other frustration-release activities. The situation spirals as continual barking or whining leads to complaints and possibly eviction. Destructive chewing can cause an apartment dweller to forfeit an expensive damage deposit, not to mention the loss of personal belongings.

If you live in an apartment you should carefully consider which rooms the dog will have access to when you are gone. Some owners may need to train their dogs to eliminate on papers in the bathroom, so this door will have to be propped open. Otherwise, if the pet accidentally shuts the door during the day, you may find your living room "bombed" with feces when you return. A variation on this same theme is the dog who locks itself in the bathroom, and proceeds to eat towels, soap, and the door in its frustration. We once had a client who complained of both problems on an every-other-day basis, until she went to a hardware store and got a good door stop!

In apartment buildings, most bathroom and kitchen pipes and ventilation systems connect to upper and lower floors. The dog that barks in the kitchen, bangs its tail on the bathroom radiator, or yodels in the living room will probably disturb several residents of an apartment complex. The terrace is no place for an unsupervised dog. Some city owners train their dogs to eliminate on a terrace, sending fumes, aromas, and even droppings down or across to their neighbors. Others use the terrace for exercise, and run the risk of the dog's falling or even hurling itself over the railing.

Correction of these problems can be difficult, regardless of the techniques used, since, in some cases, the dog simply cannot tolerate the city environment and meet its demands. Obedience training, at least to the heel, sit, stay, and come level, is always imperative. Efforts to screen city noise can be made and it might be helpful to leave the radio or TV turned on. Boredom and loneliness can be alleviated by a program of roadwork, exercise, massage, grooming, and proper diet, as described in several sections of this book. The possibility of providing a companion for the dog might also be explored. Don't think automatically in terms of another dog — a cat may be a possibility, if the two are compatible. A bird which sings or can be taught to talk is another possibility.

Dogs who must face long periods of time alone should be greeted and left calmly. The owner should not make good-byes dramatic or prolonged, pleading with the dog not to chew or bark. When the owner returns, the dog should be greeted simply but affectionately. Overdramatic hellos and good-byes often keep dogs on edge. After the owner leaves, the dog is still excited from being petted and cuddled, and possibly pleaded with to "be good." The owner may leave feeling better, but the dog may be on the edge of emotional collapse. Greeting and leaving scenes must not be the high points of the dog–owner relationship.

To burst into the house or apartment laden with special treats and then effusively greet the dog may be alleviating some of your own guilt over leaving the animal isolated, but it's a disservice to the dog. The dog's psychological alarm clock tells it when to expect the owner home. The dog gears itself up for the happy moment, the treats, the play session. If, by chance, the owner is late, as is often the case because of subway, bus, or traffic delays, the dog's anticipation can turn into frustration, and its frustration into destructiveness, whining, or barking.

If you live in a city and experience any of these problems, begin immediately to reconstruct your hello and good-bye scenes. Obedience training will help you to gain a leadership role over the dog. Even-keeled hellos and good-byes should give the dog a sense of purpose. For instance, say "Watch the house," or some such phrase as you leave. When you return, praise the dog with a cheery hello, but don't fall all over it. When you leave, offer the dog its favorite toy. When you return, delay feeding the dog for one half hour or more. If you return from work at five-thirty and feed the dog right away, you are helping to condition the dog to expect food at that time. Then the dog is frustrated whenever you are delayed and arrive home later.

SELECTING A PUPPY
FOR CITY LIFE

If you are about to select a puppy or older dog for life in the city, you should seriously consider the personality traits of different breeds. It might appear that a German shepherd dog is ill-prepared for city life, while a poodle would do well. But this is not always the case. A happy city life depends on the individual dog. Since breeders are very conscious of the rising need for dogs as protectors and companions in urban areas, many of them are selectively breeding dogs that can take city stress and adapt to the urban environment. For instance, German shepherds from certain bloodlines (The Caralon's Hein vom Lockenheim line, for example) can adapt well to city life, but others cannot. Some poodles may do well in a city environment, but others do not. It's a good idea to talk to a breeder who is breeding for pets with a high threshold for noise, low excitability, and high trainability.

On the other hand, breeders can manipulate genetics only to a certain point. Borzois are hounds that love to gallop, so they will always need an opportunity to run, which may be hard to find in the city. Malamutes, Siberian huskies and other northern breeds may never adapt to the summer heat level in a busy metropolis or be able to resist digging an occasional cooling hole. While *individuals* within a breed may adapt well, breed characteristics should still play a role in your selection of a city pet. Don't be fooled by size. Though the Doberman is a hefty dog, most Doberman blood-lines produce excellent city dogs. The Pembroke Welsh corgi, technically classed as a Working dog, is "apartment size" but very active and it may need an extraordinary amount of exercise.

To select a city dog properly, first decide objectively on your breed. Next, try to find someone who has a dog of that breed in your city. This may take some searching, or it may be as simple as stopping to chat with someone walking the kind of dog you want. Most national breed organizations will be happy to refer you to breeders specializing in city pets, or to owners of urban dogs. It is well worth your time and trouble to meet a well-adjusted city dog and owner in person and to talk over breed characteristics and potential troubles. Most breeders and dog owners will enjoy the opportunity to talk about their dogs.

It is possible to have a happy, healthy dog in the city — but it takes twice as much dedication. There is a tendency to look at dogs in terms of the services they render their owners. Whether that service be protection, companionship, or an aid to status, the function the dog serves is always secondary to the quality of the dog–owner relationship. The dog must feel responsible to, not for, its owner. It should perceive the owner as a helper and leader. The owner should act as the Alpha-figure in the dog's life. If the dog and owner's relationship is marked by affection, regard, and love, the dog will return the favor with characteristic steadfastness, respect, and friendship — regardless of where it lives.

14 Suburban Life

The suburbs may be the best of dog worlds, but its environment poses its own special set of problems. While suburban dogs are usually not as restricted, regulated, isolated, and controlled as those in the cities, the very lifting of these restrictions provides a set of pressures for the suburban dog owner.

When suburbs do have leash laws, residents do not always obey them. In general, enforcement of leash laws is lax in the suburbs. The law may include a stipulation that the dog must be leashed or "under the owner's direct control." Having a dog under one's "direct control" is, of course, an ambiguous phrase. What it means in practice is that the dog is allowed to run free but eventually returns home. This is enough "control" for some owners. Free-roving dogs often form packs or bite, a growing problem in many suburbs and villages. This is forcing suburbs to adopt city-type leash laws and implement zoning restrictions that penalize all dog owners. At least in cities, most stray dogs are picked up promptly and impounded. As a result, city dog owners tend to keep their dogs supervised, since they stand a very real chance of losing them if they don't.

Regardless of the environment, the only complete solution to free-roving is somehow to contain the dog on one's own property when it is not on leash. The best and most humane way is to bring the dog into the house where it belongs regardless of the owner's interpretations to the contrary. Assuming the dog is indoors at least fifty percent of the time and is obedience-trained to come when called, there will be little or no problem of its going off its own property. When there is a problem, secondary backup solutions are to fence in the yard or to chain the dog, an unhappy alternative.

Some suburbanites persist in believing the myth that their environment is "countryish" enough to allow their pet to go where it pleases. (Unfortunately, even a country environment does not allow that.) The suburbs are not the country, and even if they were, that is no excuse for letting a dog run wild.

Many a suburban dog owner experiencing house-soiling, chewing, digging, or free-roving has asked us if we would like to adopt a mascot for our monastic community. Aside from the fact that we already have enough dogs of our own and are responsible for ten, sometimes twenty, boarding dogs, a country life here is not the solution to the dog's problems. Dog owners cannot do without having complete control over their dog. A dog will come when it is kept close by, oriented to the inside of the house, and formally practiced in coming when called. Keep your dog inside, and either accompany it under supervision or leash it for defecation and exercise. If you want it to run free, take it to a park or large field and personally watch the dog.

Another common suburban dilemma occurs when dogs are left alone all day while the owner works. These dogs are left either inside or out and they quickly develop problems like overbarking, frustration chewing, or fence-jumping. Often they are enticed by other suburban dogs who are not restricted. It is difficult for a male dog to resist fence-jumping if a constant parade of females in season passes his way while naïve owners think their females are out doing their business. Some suburban dogs stay in yards that are fenced in but have a full view of a neighboring dog's yard. The result can be a virtual day-long bark-fest between two or more of these animals. Remember, if one dog can see another but can't get to it, barking or whining at the other animal is the usual result. In fact, regardless of whether any other dog is in sight, any arrangement for keeping the dog that includes barrier frustration (cages, pens, chains, clothesline tethers) runs the risk of producing overbarking.

The installation of a dog door, giving the dog access to both the inside and outside, often resolves these problems. If a door cannot be installed, try to screen the dog from disturbing stimuli, whether other dogs, traffic, or passersby. Ideally, a good dog should be able to stay in the house without exploding at every different sight or sound. If this is not the case, it's the owner's responsibility to seek out training to help the dog cope.

Clients often look amazed when we suggest a dog door. Won't that encourage burglars? they ask. Possibly, but a window or regular door can encourage robbers, too. A small opening obviously meant for a dog does not entice most burglars. Naturally, they are wary of households with dogs, and the dog door advertises that you have one. With a dog door the dog can defend both inside and outside areas. The expense of a dog door is minimal compared to its benefits. Some models can be installed even on rented properties, since the cutout section of door or wall can be reinserted.

There is nothing wrong with chaining a dog for a period of time for elimination, but leaving a dog on a chain all day is bound to produce undesirable results. A chain is a last resort. The ideal suburban setup, which can be used if the owner is home or away, is a small enclosed pen, preferably connected to the interior of the house by a dog door. The floor of the pen should be grass or gravel. Converting a concrete patio into a dog yard is all right, but concrete can give the dog trouble with its pads, so check them often if your dog stays on concrete for any length of time. Use creativity in constructing your pen (see Chapter 25 on canine incarceration).

Some suburban dog owners experience troubles with many of the dogs in their immediate area. A highly successful approach is to start a local obedience class together using this book and other references. (For those interested, Winifred Strickland's *Obedience Class Instruction for Dogs* is specifically geared for this.) In this way, area dogs come to regard all local adults as Alpha-figures and the troubles that ganged-up or individual suburban dogs can get themselves into decrease. If you cannot secure the co-operation of dog owners in such a project, you can at least talk to other dog owners about the value of keeping their dogs supervised. Remember, the old saying, "Love me, love my dog," applies here — you will have to be tactful in discussing dog problems with neighbors.

In suburbs where there are not enough fences and far too many dogs, fighting becomes a frequent event. Since many dogs are jammed together in a small area, each dog's territorial boundaries are frustrated. The only sensible approach is for all dog owners to obedience-train their dogs, limit defecation to the area surrounding the house, and limit free-roving.

A suburban setting can provide a wonderful life for a dog. But the owner must remember that many other dogs rub shoulders with his dog. The suburbs are not the country, and at any rate, the country is not the answer to all canine problems, as we shall see in the next chapter.

15 Country Life

There is no doubt about it: dogs do like life in the country. Each year, thousands of dogs go on vacation with their owners. They travel to the sea-shore, to the woods, to the mountains. Many clients who live the greater part of the year in the city have told us about the amazing transformation that comes over their pet once it settles into the summer retreat. The fresh air, open space, and freedom from normal restrictions can do wonders for a dog. Dogs who live in the country all year enjoy an environment that closely resembles the milieu of their wolf ancestors.

But canine country life can have its problems too. Many potential prob-lems have to do with the fact that while life in the country is freer than life in the city or suburb, the dog still must be responsibly restricted. The "myth of the country dog" states that a dog in the country is free to come and go as it pleases, need not spend any length of time indoors, and actu-ally prefers to live outdoors. This may be true of certain rare dogs, but this is usually the owner's conception of canine liberty, not the dog's. Life in the country unfortunately allows owners to force their conception of canine happiness on their dogs more easily. We have heard many troubled urban or suburban problem-dog own-ers say, "What Fido needs is a family in the country that would take him — then he could just run all day." Trouble is, even in the country Fido can't "run all day" without getting into some kind of trouble.

William, a five-year-old golden Labrador retriever, and Duffy, his one-year-old son, belonged to a family that lived in the Vermont hills. The wife called us after both dogs had participated in killing a pig at an area farm, about three miles from their home. William was an old hand at this sort of thing, and had been responsible for several other witnessed kills, including those of several geese. Duffy was relatively new to his father's occupation, but had a history of free-roving and chasing cars. Both dogs were left out in the morning and called home around five P.M. for dinner. Attempts to recall them began to falter, however, as the two dogs managed to find "dinner" elsewhere. They began to arrive home later and later, until they eventually stayed out all night. Like the proverbial drunk, they would arrive home staggering and exhausted. When they arrived home, both dogs would go immediately to the tree where they were usually chained for punishment. They would be chained for the day and night, at which point the owner would release them, and the whole ritual would be repeated. Asked why the dogs were allowed to run free, the wife explained, "Well, we live in the country, and I didn't think there was much trouble for them to get into."

Once William and Duffy were granted entrance to the house, their behavior changed remarkably. William refrained from leading Duffy into troublesome activities, and both dogs spent much of the day napping. Exercise, however, had to be regulated on leash, since the dogs had memorized a definite route during their adventures away from home, and they occasionally felt the urge to visit their old stomping grounds. After a few weeks of obedience training, the dogs could be allowed out into the yard, and came back into the house when called.

Sarah, an eleven-month-old female Norwegian elkhound, lived in a rural area. Part of her owner's land was adjacent to a sanitary landfill. Sarah discovered the landfill when she was four months old, which is the age many puppies become more independent and begin seeking adventure away from home, if permitted to do so. Sarah loved the landfill and was observed by many motorists chomping away at leftovers and licking out empty tin cans. While the owners knew where she was, the fact didn't seem to bother them since, as the owner put it, "I want her to feel free!" Sarah's "freedom" soon led her into a bout with sarcoptic mange and a serious problem with fleas. Even after veterinary treatment, she was allowed to frequent the dump. Around her eighth month, she began menacing other dogs that visited "her" dump and began growling at motorists who left their cars to empty trash. Threatening calls from the manager of the landfill convinced the owner to control the dog, but whenever unsupervised, Sarah made for the dump.

Both of the above situations involve a misunderstanding on the part of the owner of the role of the dog in the country. The old misconception that country dogs are somehow entitled to run free is played out again and again, with disastrous consequences. William and Duffy were easily rehabilitated, by a program of obedience training and in-house living. Sarah's owners needed to learn discipline techniques to correct Sarah's aggression.

In both cases, it took time for the scent of daily markings from the dogs' urination to die down. Dogs define their territory by spreading pheromones. These are chemical substances secreted by many animals, not just dogs, and used as calling cards when communicating with members of the same species. They are passed in urine, in feces, and possibly by breath. The frequent leg-lifting of males is an attempt to mark out territory, which is later defended from invasion by other dogs and possibly humans. While more common to males, pheromone-connected aggression can take place in females also. William and Duffy had successfully staked out land within a three-mile radius as their own. They considered the livestock in that area "theirs." Sarah no doubt perceived of the landfill as an extension of her own backyard, and as she matured, she began to defend the dump as her territory.

Dogs who live in the country must limit their urination and defecation to the area immediately around the home, as they usually do in the suburbs. In the city, stools are regularly swept away, destroying the defining characteristics of pheromones. This probably eliminates a consider-

able amount of aggression between city dogs who, nevertheless, are often on leash and under the control of their owners. But in the country, a dog can mark off a large area of land and feel compelled to visit its territory each day to defend it from real or imaginary invaders. Adding the possibility that an individual dog may have low discriminatory powers and high excitability, and you have all the elements for harmful aggression.

Unless the owner is able to structure the dog's life so that it leaves its canine calling cards only in its own yard, there is little chance of curing running away, aggression, or predation. Assuming this can be successfully arranged, it becomes necessary to discover exactly where the dog is traveling. Dogs who frequently run away usually have someplace to go. Find out where. Inevitably the attraction is food, an opportunity to fight or play (or both) with other dogs, or (for males) the opportunity to breed a bitch. Occasionally, some misled human will congregate dogs by passing out food. A simple phone call can stop the handing out of tidbits, but other attractions are harder to remove. Since it is usually not possible to remove them completely, a program of strict in-house living must be inaugurated, with defecation and urination on leash until the dog reorients itself to the home environment.

If your dog is involved in predatory behavior, feasting on ducks, chickens, pigs, or even "big game" like deer or bear, your approach must be the same, with some further exploration. Predatory behavior is not always easy to prove, especially if the dog is working off its own territory. The dog may be involved in a pack, with two or three animals doing the killing and everyone taking part in the feast. Just because your dog has been sighted at the scene of a predatory incident does not mean it actually killed any other animal, but you should immediately contain the dog in its home area anyway. In most states a farmer has the right to kill any dog found molesting farm animals.

Predation that takes place in the home barnyard is more complicated. Owners who want loose dogs and free-roaming chickens to coexist are asking a lot. Chickens provoke chase and capture by dogs, with their flapping wings and cackling. Often a dog that would show no interest in a silent animal will enjoy a good chicken chase if the bird runs away and puts on a good show.

We have learned several lessons in our experiences with predation cases. First, the old saying that it is harder to cure a dog of predation once the dog has "tasted blood" seems to be true. Rehabilitation for these dogs often involves extensive work on a long line, in double-blind situations, where the dog does not know it is being observed. This calls for the skillful timing and quick response of a capable trainer. If you have a chronic predator on your hands, a dog that you can't seem to convince to eat dog food and nothing else, see a competent trainer as soon as possible. If, however, your dog has developed this habit recently, discipline and the Alpha-wolf roll-over administered as soon after a chase and/or kill as possi-

ble is highly effective. Obedience training to the come, sit, and stay level is imperative to help strengthen the owner's leadership position, which is often weak.

Some trainers have used emetics effectively, lacing the "kill" with ipecac or other substances that will cause vomiting, but we have not seen much success with this method. The use of electric shock by amateurs to cure predation is to be avoided since it calls for split-second timing and is potentially dangerous.

Most predators perceive of themselves as the leader of the pack, a basic misperception that must be cleared up quickly. The dog–owner relationship needs to be effectively reordered, with the human as leader, and the dog's freedom restricted to its immediate territory. In cases of home predation, physical discipline under the chin or with the shakedown method, followed by the Alpha-wolf roll-over, is usually successful. Naturally, the cooperation of neighbors should be secured, so that they understand the problem and will call you immediately upon sighting the dog away from home. Running away and predatory behavior are avoidable if the country dog owner simply keeps his dog near.

An often successful and highly practical solution to the problems of country dogs is to put the dog to work. A great many breeds can be taught to herd sheep or cattle. There are books that describe how to home-train your dog for farm work. Hunting dogs and pointers can learn hunting skills. If you don't have a farm, there are still small tasks your dog can do. Sled dogs can be harnessed and taught to pull children around for rides. Draft dogs like Rottweilers can be harnessed to wagons and transport loads. Bringing in the paper, baby-sitting, and home protection are canine chores most dogs are eager to perform. The city dog must learn to heel with precision and to mingle with strangers peacefully; the suburban dog needs to know obedience commands and take its place as a member of the family; the country dog, too, has its special role. The fact that it lives in the country does not mean it is on a perpetual vacation, free from the restrictions and duties other dogs face. Like any dog, it needs affection, training, a sense that it belongs and is wanted. In short, the dog needs to be and feel *included*, not excluded, whether it lives on Park Avenue or in Podunk.

16 Outdoor Life

Much of the advice in this book suggests that the dog with behavior problems be moved immediately into the house. We further suggest that owners wishing to enhance their relationship with their pet, even in the absence of behavior troubles, include the dog as much as possible in their regular social life. The sections on canine sleeping habits, digging, chewing, aggression, and other problems make it clear that we feel dogs belong in the owner's "den" (house or apartment) as an integral part of a "pack" (family group) under the supervision of a pack leader or "Alpha-figure" (the dog's owner[s]). Our own lifestyle with our dogs illustrates this belief.

What about the dog that lives outside? The first question we ask is "Why?" When we ask clients who are experiencing behavior problems this question, their answers can often be dogmatic and curt:

Because I *want* him outside, that's why.

He likes it outside.

That's where a dog belongs.

He house-soils inside.

He chews (or digs, jumps up, doesn't obey) if he's inside.

I don't want hair all over the house.

He bothers company and we have a lot of company.

He needs the fresh air and exercise.

We did it with our old dog and it worked.

Occasionally there may be significant reasons for keeping a dog outside on an exclusive basis. There may be an allergy in the family, or an elderly or handicapped person in residence. As any dog owner knows, certain sacrifices must be made to keep a dog. Hair on the furniture and floors is a reality of life with a dog, as is an occasional accident. It is a rare dog that needs exercise or fresh air twenty-four hours a day.

If your dog must live outside, provide it with a large yard and a good dog house. The dog house should be wood and painted a light color in summer and a dark color in winter. The color of your dog house will affect its interior temperature. The floor of the dog house should be carpeted or otherwise insulated. Cedar shavings are good for warmth. Outdoor dogs need more fat in their diet when the temperature drops down into the forties or lower. The most convenient method is to add a tablespoon of vegetable oil to the daily diet.

But most often a dog lives outside for one of two reasons: its owners prefer it that way and see no reason to change the dog's life-style, or the dog has been tried indoors and was too unruly. If the second reason is the excuse, we hope this book will guide you in coping with behavior problems so that your dog can reenter your living quarters. If you simply prefer (or demand, as the case may be) that the dog live outdoors, there is probably no changing your mind.

Our advice to such owners faced with behavior problems is to *try* the dog in the house for one week. Expect the first couple days to be hectic. Let the dog sleep in your bedroom. If this is strictly out of the question, we suggest a limited program of obedience training done outdoors. Remember, no guarantees can be made about changing behavior that is related to social isolation, unless the dog is no longer banished. Owners who are absolutely intransigent about letting the dog into the house, even on a limited basis, might do well to consider placing the dog elsewhere and investing in a domestic animal that adapts more easily to life outdoors — for instance, a horse, a cow, or a pig.

Sensitivity
Exercises

17 Your Dog May Be Lonely

We hear a lot about America's pampered pet population these days, but such pets are in the minority. Dr. Benjamin Hart, a professor of veterinary medicine at the University of California at Davis, remarks, "Ninety-nine percent of pets aren't pampered." And he adds, "If your dog is tearing up the place, he could be lonely or he could need more exercise."* Can dogs experience loneliness? Quite easily, suggests Dr. Michael Fox, whose research indicates that the "emotional centers" of the dog's brain are similar to human emotional centers.† Recently, psychologist James L. Lynch, while studying human loneliness, conducted a series of animal experiments. Among other findings, they showed that petting could produce profound effects on the cardiovascular system of dogs.‡

One of the biggest obstacles to healthy pet–owner relationships is pet loneliness. Dog owners, busy with their own activities, may never suspect that their friend suffers from isolation. A case in point: Sassy, an Airedale terrier, spent the hours between eight and five at home, alone. Her owners worked and there were

no children in the family. She was purchased when she was four months old. Her owners were concerned that a younger puppy would not be able to adjust to long waiting periods alone. "Now we realize we should have purchased an even older, trained dog, used to entertaining itself alone," the distraught wife confessed. The ensuing conversation focused on the age of the dog, and how this was to blame for the destruction the pet wreaked when the owners were gone. But after a week's observation, we noticed that Sassy responded well to four- or five-hour periods of isolation, entertaining herself with toys, napping, and looking out windows. She was not tense or anxious, but became so after six or seven hours. We were able to observe the dog through a one-way window. While her owners had complained of Sassy's lack of pizazz and spirit, on our turf she was exuberant and playful.

In our next interview with Sassy's owners, we explored new areas. Sassy rarely left the house. She had been in a car twice, the first time when she was brought home from the breeding kennel, and the second time for a visit to a vet. While the owners rarely had guests in their own home, they were active socially and went out often at night, leaving Sassy alone for a second period of time. Questions about play periods, obedience training, fetch games, and roughhousing elicited puzzled stares from the owners. The

---

*Dr. Benjamin Hart, quoted in Associated Press dispatch, *The Boston Globe*, August 1977.

†Dr. Michael Fox, *Integrative Development of Brain and Behavior in the Dog* (Chicago: University of Chicago Press, 1971).

‡James L. Lynch, *The Broken Heart: The Medical Consequences of Loneliness* (New York: Basic Books, 1977).

situation was becoming clear: Sassy was lonely, and vented her frustration toward the end of long periods alone. Because she had been conditioned not to expect play periods or extra attention, her sullenness and lack of animation had become a generalized condition.

We suggested a daily play session, with both owners on all fours. Advising against overemotional hello or good-bye scenes, we nonetheless suggested a meal about one half hour after arriving home. To bring Sassy into contact with more people, we recommended obedience training, so that Sassy could be included in shopping trips, outings, and, if possible, parties and get-togethers with neighbors.

Sassy recovered quickly, and the destruction stopped. Weeks later, the owners reported that they had arranged for alternating trips home at noon lunch breaks to take the dog for a walk. They had ceased socially overextending themselves in an effort to bolster the husband's business career, and they now reserved two nights a week to stay at home, including their dog in the family circle. They began to host parties at home, taught Sassy standard obedience work and some parlor tricks, and showed her off to friends. They stopped excluding the dog from their lives, firmly integrating her into their daily schedules.

Dogs are social animals, and they need to be included in a pack. Since we have deprived them of their normal pack — animals of their own species — and the freedom to set up social structures of their own, we must include them in *our* pack and help them to adapt to human social structures. Because so many of us are simply out of touch with our own animality, and even more out of touch with the kingdom of animals, our initial reaction is to deny animals entrance to our human world. The old dichotomies of good and evil, body and spirit, animal and man, are still played out dramatically in pet–owner relationships.

Many pet owners perceive their charges to be incapable of enjoying human company. The tendency is to isolate dogs rather then include them. Although dogs are allowed in supermarkets and restaurants in many parts of Europe, they are barred in the United States, where they are considered a "health hazard." Shopping centers and malls now frequently forbid pets entry, on or off leash, and in some large urban areas, dogs are even being barred from city parks. The social situation for our pets promises to get worse, not better. The capital of Iceland and Roosevelt Island in New York, to mention two areas, now forbid ownership of dogs. Dogs will continue to be ostracized and isolated as long as the pet population soars and owners act irresponsibly with their dogs. What all this adds up to, from the dog's point of view, is more isolation, more boredom, and more loneliness. This, in an animal that is genetically a *pack* animal!

But there are ways of providing an enriching communal life for your dog. First of all, don't leave your dog alone if you can help it. Remember, the inbuilt tendency is to leave the dog home. But stop and reflect: can I take the dog with me? You might be able to. Second, provide varied human interaction for your dog. Obedience-train the dog to the come, sit, stay, down level. Begin to take your dog to busy streets, shopping centers (if allowed), and other people-congested areas where your dog can observe people in motion, look at neutral passersby, and in general get a feel for what it is like to be around large groups of people. If possible, extend this exposure to include family re-unions, outdoor parties, and other situations.

KEEPING YOUR DOG CLOSE

At New Skete we try to keep our dogs with us most of the time. A puppy begins by simply following the Brother in charge wherever he goes. Most puppies have a natural tendency to follow humans, and we try to maximize this inclination. New puppy owners should include a ten- or fifteen-minute session daily when they have their pup follow them, off lead, while changing pace, swooping into turns, and keeping the pup ani-mated and happy with high-intensity encouragement. This simple pro-cedure will help alleviate come-on-command problems later in life. Pup-pies who are hesitant about following their masters should be leashed and the leash attached to your belt loop. The monks here will often proceed with work that requires both hands simply by tying the pup and leash to their belt loop.

Older dogs can be taught to follow and stay close by this same method. The older the animal, the more con-ditioning on leash is required before the dog gets the idea that staying close is a pleasant experience. Owners who complain that they cannot keep their dogs with them or take them along on outings because they will run away at the first opportunity should try a few days using the leash as an umbilical cord. Needless to say, other aspects of the dog–owner rela-tionship must be in order if the dog is to learn to prefer the owner's com-pany to any other activity.

To give you an idea of how suc-cessfully a dog can be integrated into a busy schedule, let's look at two day-time rituals. The first is the schedule of a monk at New Skete, and the second is a timetable for a busy housewife we'll call Mrs. Bede:

MONK'S SCHEDULE:

6:30 A.M.   New Skete monk prepares for morning church service, attends to personal care while dog is let into out-door defecation and ex-ercise pen.

7:00 A.M.   Matins (morning prayer). Brother goes to church, his dog waits in his room or in a kennel pen. Dog is fed and left alone to eat at this time. This helps pass the time until the monk returns.

8:00 A.M.   Brother eats breakfast in monastery dining room. Dogs lie down near dining room walls until breakfast is finished.

9:00 A.M.   Work. Brother takes dog with him wherever he is working that day. He does not allow random running around, gives the down-stay command and makes the dog hold it. Brothers working in the kennels or at training have their dogs tag along. Office workers tuck their dogs under the desk. Work in the church can be done with the dogs lying down in the sacristy. At the inspected butcher shop, dogs lie outside the door.

12 noon Monks eat lunch. While the Brothers eat, dogs lie down nearby as at breakfast. No begging or coming to the table is allowed.

1:00 P.M. Afternoon work period. Same as morning work period for both monks and dogs.

3:00 P.M. Some Brothers continue working, while others take their dogs for walks, give them obedience lessons, or give them a siesta time.

6:00 P.M. Same as above for meals.

7:30 P.M. Vespers. Brothers go to church, dogs wait in rooms. Some dogs fed again at this time.

8:30 P.M. Dogs attend community meetings or recreation with monks. Community of brothers relates with colony of dogs.

approx. Brothers retire with dogs
9:30 P.M. to their rooms to read, prepare for sleep.

On weekends, there are more church services, and more free time. On Sunday, the dogs mingle with the crowds who attend church at New Skete or come to visit in the afternoon.

MRS. BEDE'S SCHEDULE:

7:00 A.M. Rises, prepares breakfast for children, takes dog from her bedroom and puts dog outside in enclosed yard to take care of its needs. Helps prepare for school.

8:00 A.M. Dog accompanies children to nearby bus stop. Mrs. Bede calls dog back home immediately after bus departs. Dog eats.

9:00 A.M. Dog watches indoors as Mrs. Bede attends to housework.

11:00 A.M. Shopping trip. Mrs. Bede loads dog and two preschoolers into car. Dog stays in the car while she shops.

12 noon Dog lies by table as Mrs. Bede prepares lunch for preschoolers and herself.

1:00 P.M. Children nap. Dog takes nap in children's room at same time. Mrs. Bede naps or does ironing, other housework.

3:00 P.M. Two children return from school; dog instinctively goes to door to be let out to meet bus.

3:15 P.M. Children and dog return from school, have snack in kitchen. Children have play session in backyard with dog. After half an hour dog called in and confined.

4:30 P.M.   Mrs. Bede gives dog fifteen-minute obedience session in backyard, includes children in training session.

4:45 P.M.   Mrs. Bede prepares dinner with dog on down-stay in kitchen.

5:30 P.M.   Mr. Bede returns home, goes jogging with dog.

6:30 P.M.   Family eats, with dog on down-stay near table.

7:30 P.M.   Dog recreates, watches TV, etc., with family.

10:45 P.M.   Dog taken outside to eliminate.

11:00 P.M.   Dog retires in master bedroom for the night.

Notice that both these schedules keep the dog near its master. The dog is included, not excluded. The dog is almost always *with people*, although one or two private rest periods are included in both schedules, timed with human rest periods. Similarly, when humans are taking care of their personal needs, dogs are too. The dogs are left alone to eat, contrasting with the "Grand Central Station" atmosphere of many pets' eating time. Periods of exercise are included. The dog is treated as a true companion and friend, part of the family circle. The dogs in these schedules are not treated as emotional cripples who need attention every minute of the day. Nor do their masters fall victim to any number of assorted dog myths — for instance, the myth that a dog needs to run free eighty percent of the day.

To prevent canine loneliness and the possible destruction and neurotic behavior that can stem from it, integrate the dog into your schedule. Take time to map out your schedule, seeing how you can include the dog in it. Don't assume that your dog is automatically eliminated from certain activities or areas — ask, inquire. Some owners might find it possible to take their dogs to work, if they are obedience-trained and quiet. In the best dog and owner relationships, isolation is usually the exception, rather than the rule.

18 Where Is Your Dog This Evening?

Where does your dog sleep at night? If your answer is "in the bedroom, on the floor," you probably already know the gist of this chapter. If your reply is "in the cellar," "tied in the kitchen," or "in bed, with me," read on. We will discuss here the value of "sleep therapy" for you and your dog, and how to go about it.

One objection clients have when we suggest they have their dog sleep in the bedroom involves what they conceive of as the impropriety of the situation. One client put it this way: "I tie her in the kitchen at night. That's where she's always stayed. Sometimes she'll chew overnight. Until I got a steel tether, she used to chew right through the leather one until she got free. Then she would run into the bedroom. She would creep in and I would discover her the next morning. So I began to shut the kitchen door. Then she learned how to open the latch on the kitchen door. So I shut the bedroom door. She began scratching on the bedroom door. What does this sound like to you?"

"It sounds like she's trying to get into the bedroom," we responded. "Did you ever consider letting her sleep in the bedroom?"

"Heavens no! My husband would never allow it. We might be in the middle of something! [Client clears her throat.] It just doesn't seem proper. But how am I going to teach her she *belongs* in the kitchen?"

Hopefully this chapter will help the woman above, and others like her, to get over a phobia about having a dog in the bedroom overnight. However, if you are absolutely determined that the dog stay out of your bedroom, perhaps you can provide comfortable alternative sleeping conditions. Though we highly recommend letting the dog sleep in the bedroom, we can see how it can be a negative experience if a nervous owner is sending out negative vibrations all night. The dog will pick these up. But if you can see the value of the experience, from the dog's point of view, and are willing to try it, you will be surprised how fast your phobias fade.

BEDROOM DEPORTMENT

Your pooch is in the room and you're ready to retire. While it is best to have trained your dog to lie down in advance (see Chapter 33, "The Down"), it is surprising how even the most hyperactive dogs will tend to plop down as soon as the lights are shut off. If your dog paces, runs around, or gets up too often, you might want to start teaching the down and tethering the dog to the foot of the bed. Allow no jumping on the bed or other horseplay. Discipline this by curtly removing the dog from the bed and literally depositing it on the floor with a sharp "No!"

Provide a spot for the dog with a small rug or blanket. Food and water are not needed overnight. The best policy is to have the dog lie down, to ignore it, and to go about preparing to retire. Do not make a fuss over the dog. This is a time of quiet, uncomplicated interaction between you and your dog. It is a time when you let the dog into your private "den" — but not to disrupt it. Most dogs will simply find a wall and lie down against it. Some like to lie under a desk since it provides a denlike atmosphere. As long as it is not inconvenient for you, let the dog pick the spot. Don't force the dog to lie anywhere. If there is an area the dog lies on that bothers you, block it off by rearranging furniture or placing an object in the way.

Finally, turn off the lights. This is usually the final sign-off. If you have problems with pacing or hyperactivity, more common in males than females, try turning off the lights and telling the dog to lie down. The majority will circle in a holding pattern for a few revolutions, and then land for the night.

GET UP!

The canine privilege of inhabiting the master's den is just that — a privilege. Don't allow your dog to abuse it. If the dog bothers you during the night, give it a slight cuff under the chin and the command to lie down. Pawing the bed or trying to get on it should result in slapped paws and the shove-off. In general, it is a good idea to keep the dog away from the top of the bed but still in the bedroom. Dog owners who enjoy a long "goodnight" scene or ritual bedroom romp are inviting trouble and canceling out the potential benefits that stem from an in-bedroom sleep. Don't go overboard. Allow your dog to share your den, but not take it over.

If your dog bothers you during the early morning hours, it may be obeying its psychological and physical alarm clock that tells it to defecate. If your dog has a regular schedule for elimination, you will need to stick to this, regardless of whether you want to sleep in. Many a dog owner has become an expert at stumbling to the door on a Saturday morning, letting the dog out and back in, then falling back into bed for a little more shut-eye. Part of being a dog owner is respecting your dog's inner schedule. The more mature the dog, the more control it will have. With time, you should be able to sleep later, and the dog will too.

On the other hand, some dogs will take an invitation into the bedroom as a chance to play "doorman" with their owners. Don't get up "every hour, on the hour" for your dog. Take the dog out before retiring and make sure it has had enough time to eliminate. During the night, ignore whining and shush it with a stern "No." In the case of young puppies, you should get up and take the pup out, but older dogs can usually "hold it." Don't rev the dog up before retiring, since this might encourage vomiting or defecation.

THE VALUE OF IN-BEDROOM SLEEPING

Of all the training exercises described in this book, "sleep therapy" is the easiest. You don't have to do much except let the dog in and out of the room and keep the whole experience in the room as low-key as possible. But this is a time when a lot is happening, from the dog's point of view. The dog is enjoying an extended period of time with your scent. The bedroom contains the most intense scents. They focus on the bed itself, especially in the center of the bed. This is why we prefer that the dog not be allowed on the bed. If they allow the dog on the bed, owners may discover the middle of the mattress chewed up. Some contact with the owner's scent is beneficial, too much contact backfires. The rest of the bedroom is a fragrant delight. The closet houses shoes and socks, the rug on the floor is walked on by bare feet, and the drapes are touched constantly. For your dog, the in-bedroom sleep is a "high" — but a high that must be properly regulated and controlled.

It is a time when the owner and dog can have extended contact without demanding anything from each other. It is a time when the majority of dogs make their own decision to lie down and relax with you, to shut down, turn off, sleep. This, in itself, while deceptively uneventful, builds trust and confidence between owner and dog. Consequently the in-bedroom sleep can be a great help if you are experiencing problems with hyper-activity, social isolation, lack of rapport, night barking and whining, or general unruliness. For the owner without much time for a pet, it can be a final moment of contact and attention.

In over four hundred "problem-dog" cases we have worked with at New Skete, eighty percent of the problem dogs slept outside of the bedroom, usually in the living room, basement, outdoors, or, significantly, just outside the bedroom door.

All of the New Skete monks keep their assigned dogs in their rooms at night. The bedrooms are in the cloistered section, where we have a rule forbidding any noise. Our dogs glide into the room behind us; then we give the down command with a hand signal and go about the business of retiring. Our dogs are usually asleep before we are.

A good example of the power of in-bedroom sleeping is what happens when we have an imported dog arrive here from Germany. Since we try to include the very best bloodlines in our breeding program, some dogs must come from overseas. They may or may not know any English when they arrive, and are generally disoriented. But after a week of sleeping in the same room with one of the monks, they calm down and follow that Brother around like a shadow. This is a good tip for trainers and others who must get to know strange dogs in a short period of time in order to train them or nurse them — move them into your bedroom for sleeping and wonders occur.

DOG DREAMS

Dogs do dream. They will often be quite verbal about it, moaning and purring during the dream. Some owners have mistakenly thought the best thing to do is wake the dog up and stop the "nightmare." But the old adage "let sleeping dogs lie" applies here. If the dog's REM (rapid eye movement) sleep is disturbed too often, daytime hyperactivity and unruliness can result. If the dream becomes really noisy, try stopping it by crinkling a piece of paper or tapping the floor. This will change the pattern of the dream but not wake the dog up.

To us, it *is* important where your dog sleeps. The best place is in your bedroom, in *your* den. Needless to say, the protection potential of any pet increases insofar as it can quickly alarm its owners of any danger. If the dog has access to your bedroom, you have a built-in burglar and fire alarm.

19 Playing Pavlov

The Russian experimental psychologist Ivan Pavlov (1849–1936) used dogs extensively in his experiments with conditioned reflex. Though he was not specifically concerned with dog training, he left a body of work that can be of great value to breeders, trainers, and dog owners. This chapter does not pretend to explore all Pavlov's work, much less in detail. Nevertheless, we can and will explain a canine socialization and training technique that is highly Pavlovian in style.

A simple set of keys can help you deepen your relationship with your dog and alleviate many forms of problem behavior. Dogs with recall problems, a tendency for chewing, digging, or other destructive antics, or appetite problems can be successfully "keyed in" by a simple form of sound conditioning. You will need four or five keys on a key chain. Every second key should be brass, while the others should be made of another metal, preferably not aluminum. Brass and steel make higher-pitched sounds, and four or five keys sound better to dogs than ten or twenty.

The basic idea behind this sound conditioning is to *precede desired behavior with a distinctive sound.* Keys are used here since they provide a strong, high-pitched sound that is irresistible to the dog once it is properly conditioned. Hand clapping, whistling, and cooing are in another realm, obviously proceeding from a person. To these specifically human

A simple set of keys can help alleviate problems.

sounds, a dog may or may not respond, depending on the current state of the relationship between the dog and the person making the sound. Keys or whistles are neutral, and therefore more effective. In our experience, however, we find the most effective sound device to be the keys on a chain.

Let's take an example. Your dog doesn't come when called. If you have a puppy or a dog under two years old, your chances for effective sound conditioning to correct the "come problem" are better than with an older dog who is used to going the other way when called. Yet, it is never too late to try this training technique. For the utmost success, you must have regular feeding times for your dog twice daily, and he must finish eating in about fifteen to twenty minutes. If you have your dog on the "nibbler

plan" you will have to switch to regular feeding times and remove the food if it is not finished promptly. (We suggest this method of feeding in general.) Before placing the dish within his reach and allowing him to eat, get your dog's attention and jingle the keys for two or three seconds. Then go about your business as he eats. Do not make a show out of this, and preferably do not allow your dog to see you jingle the keys. You may attach the keys to your belt loop with a snap belt. Repeat this procedure at the second meal, continuing it for two or three weeks. Do not use the keys around your dog for any other purpose until you have spent some time in this conditioning procedure whenever your dog eats. Another positive booster and "reinforcing effect" can be gained by using the keys whenever you return from work, from an errand, or in your car — stop the motor, open the door (both distinctive sounds in themselves), jingle the keys, and call out the dog's name in a happy voice that carries.

After two or three weeks, begin a daily session in which you call your dog, jingle the keys, and praise him lavishly when the recall is good. Make sure you are *crouching down*, have a smile on your face, have your arms open to "funnel" the dog in to you, and are not overjingling your keys. The whole point, obviously, is to let the dog hear the sound of the keys — the conditioning sound — so that he reacts positively, on his own. Let the dog win. Then reverse the procedure by jingling first and then calling your dog's name. Finally, try it with the keys alone. Above all, make sure your praise is animated, verbal, and physical when your dog comes to you. There is hardly a moment in training more deserving of praise than the successful recall. (*Never*, by the way, call a dog to you and then discipline it. If you have any other than a happy reception planned for your dog at the end of a come-in, *go and get the dog yourself*.)

Remember that sound conditioning for recall is a training technique that builds on itself. You must keep it up at mealtime and expand the principle to other happy occasions such as treats, play sessions, or car trips. Always follow up the key jingling with a *happy* experience.

Key therapy works on a group level, too. Puppies are often sound conditioned in lieu of giving them names since the breeder may prefer to leave the prerogative to the future owner. Since it is so effective with puppies and younger dogs, keys can help teach pups recall, can aid in gait evaluation, and will help keep a litter grouped and diverted from traffic and other dangers. One breeder detoured a litter of nine puppies from a busy highway with a few jingles of her trusty keys. Some professionals also use the key method to *double-handle* dogs in the show ring. In double-handling, one handler actually shows the dog, while the double-handler provides ringside encouragement, often with strategic key jingling. However, we should note that this is a technique forbidden by the American Kennel Club though it is the subject of much debate and is practiced widely.

For dogs with appetite problems, begin as above, jingling your keys a couple of times before placing the food before your dog. Pavlov's dogs salivated at the sound of the bell, and the principle here is just the same. Appetite problems often have many roots (see Chapter 11 on feeding), so make sure that if your pet is already playing a food game with you, you are not simply adding the key ritual without correcting the basic trouble first.

Chewers, diggers, and general house-wreckers can sometimes be diverted from their destructive activities by strategic sound therapy. Verbal or physical discipline is the usual corrective for this kind of behavior, but the dog that fails to respond to these methods may respond to sound diversion. Keys, whistles, and other sound devices are especially helpful with dogs who chew or dig when the owner is absent.

Here is just such a case.

Thunder, a two-year-old malamute, spent the day digging holes in the backyard. When the owners returned, it was standard procedure to wallop the dog and then isolate him. The digging, however, continued to get worse until, in exasperation, they went to their veterinarian who referred them to us. Thunder appeared to be a normal, sound male, alert and active, with some holdover behavior from puppyhood. We combined a program of basic obedience training, some diet changes, and sound conditioning. Later, when Thunder left us, his owners began to condition the dog with a simple key set at mealtimes, early morning and at night. The dog's mistress had a sick day off and she spent the day at a neighbor's house which had a view of her backyard. Using the keys, she anticipated digging and jingled the keys several times that afternoon. She had provided other objects for Thunder. Balls, sticks, and play toys had previously offered no diversion to the digging. Construction of a simple "obstacle course" of old tires and boards, and some large tree limbs, did. When she returned to work the next day, she left the keys with her neighbor, who agreed to watch for signs of canine excavation. This helpful neighbor jingled the keys whenever she felt the dog was about to begin digging or if she actually caught the dog in the act. By the end of two weeks' time, with the combined impact of many facets of our program, the digging had stopped completely. The owner now considered installing a dog door to give the animal the option of being inside or out. Previously, she was against this, fearing in-house destruction more than the outdoor variety. Later, she reported that neighbors had observed that the dog spent about fifty percent of the time indoors, and that there was no destruction of any kind, in or out.

The following is an instance wherein sound conditioning stopped uncontrolled barking in the owner's absence. Shana, a year-old collie-shepherd mix, barked and squealed incessantly while her owner was at work. This vocalizing began about an hour after the owner's departure, as neighbors reported in their complaints to the landlord who thereupon threatened eviction. In exploring the dog's life-style, we found that the owner put the dog on edge each morning with a prolonged emotional good-bye scene, comforting the dog and begging (!) it not to bark during the day. When she left, she felt great, but the dog was left in a state of emotional exhaustion. On returning home, the owner would launch into an ecstatic greeting, hugging the dog, thanking it for being quiet (!) during the day — or relatively quiet, as the neighbor's reports would have it. We immediately cooled these rituals, thus taking some of the emotional overload off the animal. Then we began basic obedience. In this case, sound conditioning consisted of a free day spent at a neighbor's apartment *within earshot* of the dog, and with a high-pitched whistle in hand. The owner also provided three other neighbors with such whistles which they dutifully blew whenever the dog "revved up." Furthermore, the owner also spent a day *in hiding* with another approach. When Shana began her canine speech, the owner ran down from the apartment above, burst into her own apartment, charged at the dog, disciplined her under her chin, placed her on a down, and turned her over in the classic Alpha-wolf reprimand position (see Chapter 10 on discipline). An Oscar-winning performance! The owner's excellent sense of timing, her dramatic ability, and the element of surprise gave her forceful display the exact results she wanted. The barking ceased. The owner continued to sound-condition her dog at mealtimes with a whistle. (The whistle, by the way, was used in this case rather than the keys since the sound of the former would readily pierce the apartment walls.) We retained the sound conditioning as a backup measure in case the barking should resume, and because it had been useful on other levels in the dog–owner relationship, such as recall and appetite problems.

A simpler problem was exemplified in the case of a two-year-old German shepherd, Abbey, a lovely bitch of show quality. She was being campaigned to her championship, having already completed obedience work to CDX level. She had no trouble mixing the different types of work demanded in the obedience and conformation rings, but she had one slight problem. When anyone proffered a camera to take a show shot, her ears went down, her tail flipped inward, and her expression became dull and forlorn. Here, too, sound conditioning won the day. In all such picture-taking sessions, a second person would stand before her out of camera range and "bait" her with the keys; Abbey's whole demeanor would change, allowing highly animated, attractive photographs.

Pavlov's initial discoveries can be expanded with great success in dog behavior modification. If you have questions about sound therapy for dogs, it is best to consult a trainer experienced in applying it. Pavlov's lectures on conditioned reflex make interesting, if heavy, reading.* Playing Pavlov can be fun and effective, limited only by your ability to understand and apply the basic principles of sound conditioning.

20   Silence and Your Dog

Animals are creatures that lead silence through the world of man and language and are always putting silence down in front of man. Many things that human words have upset are set at rest again by the silence of animals. Animals move through the world like a caravan of silence.

A whole world, that of nature and that of animals, is filled with silence. Nature and animals seem like protuberances of silence. The silence of animals and the silence of nature would not be so great and noble if it were merely a failure of language to materialize. Silence has been entrusted to the animals and to nature as something created for its own sake.

— Max Picard, *The World of Silence*

Once, an Irish Setter named Queenie was brought to us, quivering like a leaf. The harried housewife wanted to leave her with us for observation. "She shakes like that all the time," she explained; "I don't know if she can take our life-style." This comment

* I. P. Pavlov, *Conditioned Reflexes,* trans. G. V. Anrep (London: Oxford University Press, 1927).

inaugurated a discussion of the lifestyle at the dog's home. The woman described her family as "active" and "robust" — and, she added, "very noisy." Meanwhile, three preschoolers were in the car in the parking lot, alternately laughing, screaming, and crying. When asked if she wanted the children to be in on the consultation, the woman exclaimed, "Oh no, they're too noisy. When they're around, Queenie shakes even more!"

As we explored the family situation, it became clear that this dog had hardly any time to itself. Except for a five-hour stretch during which she slept, the poor animal lived under a constant barrage of noise and racket. Orders and requests in this family, whether to the dog or to each other, were screamed or shouted. The television was the heartbeat of the home and was on almost twenty-four hours a day, even if no one was watching it. When the family went out somewhere, the TV and radio were left blaring because they were afraid Queenie might become lonely and launch out on a spree of destruction. Furthermore, the home was situated on a busy highway, and this lent its own noise to what the family produced.

However, Queenie's problem of shaking had only started when she was six months old. The family had purchased the dog when she was two months old, and the animal had been fine for about four months. But once the shakes had started, they had continued, and now Queenie was almost two. In all her time with these people, she had enjoyed few moments alone (even defecation was on a leash).

After two days in our relatively quiet surroundings, she stopped shak-

Brothers John and Nil take a silent walk in the woods with their dogs. (Photograph by Sister Theresa Mancuso)

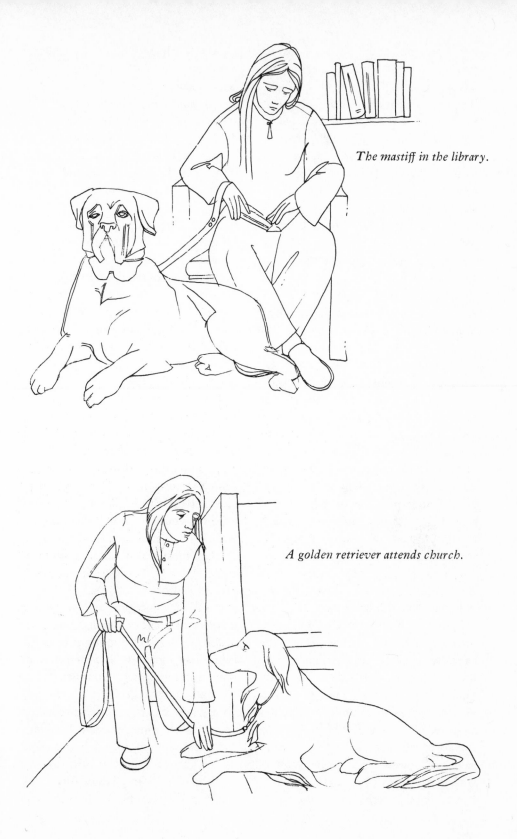

The mastiff in the library.

A golden retriever attends church.

ing. The problem did not appear to be genetic, nor did it seem to stem from any kind of high-strung nervousness. Trained in a park obedience program, she responded to normally spoken commands and even to whispered instructions. While with us, she seemed to enjoy herself thoroughly. She entertained herself by tossing balls, by sprinting, and by relating to her canine neighbors in our kennels. When the owners came to pick her up, they could not believe the transformation.

After suggesting some diet changes and a vet check, we then launched into a discussion of home conditions and the way the dog was treated. We emphasized daily obedience exercises, daily play sessions, and, most important, some quiet time alone for Queenie. As a result of reexamining this whole situation, the owners stopped blaming the dog for not being able to "take it" and began to consider their own behavior and the general atmosphere in their home setting. The children (this time included in the discussion) were especially sensitive and concerned. One boy, five, said he often had headaches all day. Pointing to their pet he said, "Maybe Queenie does, too."

Yes, dogs need silence. They need some time alone, even though they are basically pack-oriented animals, and it's up to us to provide them with some quiet time. Though most obedience sessions should be highly animated and lively, full of peppy talk and encouragement, it's a good idea to have an occasional quiet session, whispering the commands, moving around lightly, perhaps even conduct-

ing the whole period in a wooded area or a park. Eye contact, also, works with silence as essential elements in any good canine–human relationship. It's a good practice to stop once a day, get your dog's attention, and simply look at him. However, don't stare. Simply stop, look, and smile, while remaining silent. In a word, "insee," as Rilke says. Then end this moment with an affectionate pat or friendly word. Direct stares, hard and penetrating, can be interpreted as threatening, so avoid them. The kind of silent eye contact we are concerned with here is gentle and sustained, a real exchange between animal and man, and therefore its entire "tonality" is one of peace and quiet.

There is a myth that all obedience training should be done in noisy environments that simulate "real life." There *is* a point here, and distractions and other noise serve to teach proper retention of commands. But especially at the beginning of formal training, you must plan a silent session with your dog. Silence is such a rarity that we must plan for it or it will not come our way. So figure it into your life, and into your dog's life. Everyone has at some time experienced a moment of silent communication with his or her dog. It's important to cultivate these moments as you grow in your relationship with your pet.

Some city dwellers might well ask, "But where can I go for silence every day?" With some creative thinking, there are solutions. One urbanite takes his obedience-trained mastiff to the local branch library. He explained his situation to the head librarian and asked for a trial run. Another woman in a crowded suburban area stops at a local church for ten minutes every day and puts her golden retriever on a down-stay between the pews. Still another owner closes his windows to highway noise, draws the drapes, lights a candle, and does yoga while his dog lies nearby. The gist is obvious; if there are already quiet reflective moments in your life, it is just a matter of letting your dog in on them. If, on the other hand, you never have any quiet time alone to retreat and refocus yourself, perhaps you should think of ways to incorporate some such moments into your own life and share them with your dog.

21 Radio Training

One piece of equipment in our training collection that looks out of place when lined up with training collars and leashes is the radio. You can use a radio to help train your dog. All you need to do is tune in a station.

Playing the radio for a litter of puppies is an old breeder's socialization technique. Some of us play the radio for our puppies here at New Skete. Since we are an all-male community, and since most of our puppies go into a family setting, we feel it is important for them to hear female voices. Barbara Walters's nightly newscast has been heard by many of our pups. During the day, they may listen to talk shows featuring housewives calling in helpful homemaking hints. Call-in talk shows offer a wide and constantly changing variety of voices. But stay away from "controversial" shows that feature people arguing.

Some say rock is the best socialization music for pups, and others swear by classical music. The positive effects of Beethoven on dairy cow milk production is well known by farmers. In the movie *One Flew Over the Cuckoo's Nest* mental patients were lulled into inertia by "easy-listening" music that was played all the time. As far as we know, no specific studies have been done on the effects of different types of music on dogs, but it is our experience that music can be of value for dogs. Be careful not to bombard the dog with noise. But do use the radio creatively, especially for problems.

The radio can help a dog spend long periods of time alone. An example: Clancy, a two-year-old Irish setter, had difficulty staying alone while his owner, a young office worker, was at work. He barked incessantly. The desperate secretary brought the dog in for training after her neighbors threatened to have her evicted if the barking did not stop. Clancy began obedience training right away, mastering heel, sit, stay, and come very quickly. His owner remarked during one session how attentive Clancy was to the sound of popular records played on the stereo. "The first thing I do when I get home is put on a stack of records to help me unwind. Clancy loves it. He sits right next to the speakers and listens, almost like the famous RCA Victor dog."

This tip helped us to figure out an additional tactic to stop the barking. We instructed the owner to begin playing the radio a half hour before leaving home, and to leave the radio on all day, on a station featuring the kind of music she usually played when returning home. She should continue to play the radio or stereo when she returned home. Greetings and departures were to be kept low-key. Combined with obedience training, the radio format seemed to help the setter keep quiet. The radio masked traffic and street noises that may have helped set the dog off on a barking spree, especially the sound of children and other dogs playing in a nearby school yard.

Looking back on the Clancy case, we reflected that many breeders and boarding-kennel proprietors use piped-in music because they feel it quiets barkers and howlers. If you consider "radio therapy" for your dog, don't rely on it as the only technique to solve barking or other problems. It will need to be combined with an effective program of obedience training. Don't forget that too much noise can backfire. Remember the story of Queenie in the last chapter!

22 Massage for Dogs

Every culture that allows domestic pets teaches its members ways to relate physically with those pets. In some Moslem countries dogs live a dog's life, and are rarely held or petted. We've noticed that some German dogs that we import do not seem to like our "American" way of petting. After investigation with our German contacts, we have learned that Germans have a slightly different approach to their dogs. They pet and stroke them in a different way and in different places than do many Americans.

In our culture, petting a dog is very important. Most people tend to pet dogs around the head and shoulder regions and stop there. Others literally trounce their dogs, pounding their sides and ruffling their fur.

Begin at the dog's head, gently massaging the eyelids, muzzle, and nose.

Choose a leg and work up and down gently.

Sometimes there is little method to the physical display. The dog is expected to "take it" whether or not it is the kind of physical affection it enjoys. Few dog owners stop to read their dog's needs and desires. A dog owner may find that the dog does not enjoy being petted — if by petting we mean rough jostling or pounding. Instead, like many humans, they greatly enjoy a more extended type of body contact — a kind of massage.

Massage can be a beneficial technique when used as an aid to relaxation. The first principle of dog massage is to stop thinking of your dog solely from the shoulders up. Contact can be made with almost any part of the dog's body if it is sensitive contact. Skilled veterinarians know this from treating unapproachable patients. They often have to devise creative ways of lifting the animal up onto an examination table, or treating injuries all over a pet's body.

To begin dog massage, make a list of all the areas where a given dog likes body contact. If you are the dog's owner, you know. If you are not, ask the owner. Then list the areas where the dog is sensitive to touch. Begin your first massage with the areas on your first list, but include one area on the second. Gradually include more "forbidden" areas as you give massages. Dog massage is best done on the floor. A carpeted area is best. The immediate inclination of many dogs is to play. Don't make massage a businesslike experience. If the dog wants to play, let it play. It's best to begin on the head, gently massaging the eyelids, muzzle, and nose. Always keep one hand in contact with the dog during the entire massage. It's best to have the dog in the sitting position. From the head area, work down the neck to the chest and pectoral muscle. Some dogs will automatically offer a paw. Take hold of it, but gently place it down if the dog seems to be losing balance.

Choose a leg and work up and down on it very gently. If your dog decides to lie down, you will have better access to its rear legs. Try to avoid forcing the dog down. If your dog knows the command for down, you can use it in massage work, but don't force the issue. Make your strokes long and firm. Try to distinguish massage from regular petting. The massage should be more extended and pliable in its movement than regular petting. Avoid all slapping, pinching, and pulling motions. These will break the mood of the massage.

Many dogs will communicate quite clearly what they like and dislike. For the owner who has never had such extended contact with the pet, it may take awhile to feel comfortable. Try to drop embarrassment and timidity. If you are nervous during the massage, your dog will sense it and tighten up.

There are many benefits to dog massage. It is a veterinary technique used to hasten rehabilitation following fractures and luxations and to restore muscle tone. It can give you a new appreciation of canine anatomy. For the busy dog owner, it is a way of disciplining oneself to make contact with the pet. It is a welcome break for dogs in obedience training. For show dogs, massage is an excellent calming procedure before entering the ring,

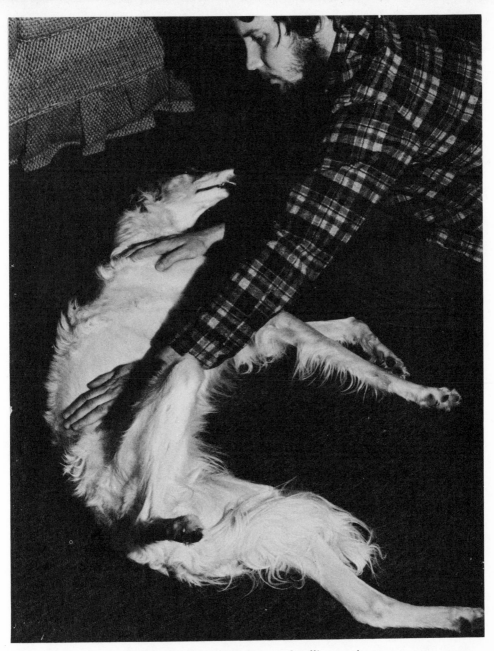

Avoid all slapping, pinching, and pulling motions.

where a delicate balance between relaxation and animation must be maintained if the dog is to look its best.

A technique for calming down a stressed dog is to place your open palm over the dog's groin area and hold it there. On females, this is just below the stomach, on males, just in front of the genital area. The groin area is a traditional greeting place between fellow canines. Dogs often tell each other "it's all right" by nudging this area. When you gently place your hand there, it has the same effect on the dog as an arm around the shoulder or a handshake can have for worried humans. Try this technique if your dog becomes agitated while at the veterinarians, when you need to groom it, cut its toenails, or anytime the dog is under stress.

We often suggest massage in the case of an overworked, overstressed, or neglectful dog–owner relationship.

Children are often great at dog massage, once they understand what it is about. It is a good substitute for unhealthy kinds of contact between kids and dogs, such as ear-pulling, chasing, and tail-yanking. For the dog owner who finds it difficult to reach his pet, especially on the verbal level, with massage he can often calm the animal down enough so that it can learn and retain commands. We have had success with "hyperkinetic" dogs by including a five- or ten-minute massage session *before* commencing regular obedience work.

23 The Round-Robin Recall

Dogs with recall problems can be helped with a simple game the whole family can play. You will need a twenty-foot rope or lead, with a light weight attached to one end. Your dog should wear a training collar and *should already be trained to the come, sit, and stay level before attempting round-robin work.*

Begin by forming a small circle of four or five people. The object of the exercise is to call the dog, have the dog sit in front of you, praise the dog, and toss the rope to the next person in the circle. This person then calls the dog and repeats the process. The tossed rope is to insure a prompt re-

call by the dog. If the dog does not come after being called twice, give the lead a sharp jerk and *call the dog as you jerk the line.* As the dog comes to each person in the circle, that person should have the dog sit and then give lavish praise.

All participants should make this a lively, fun session. It should not be a formal, precise lesson, but an experience in animation and praise. Keep the dog happy by giving encouragement. As soon as the dog is called and even looks at the caller, that person should start giving the dog encouragement. But if the dog does not come in, or begins to go the other

Call the dog, and if it does not come in right away, give a snap on the long lead. Keep sending the dog around the circle.

Toss the lead to your partner before he begins to call the dog, so that he can snap the lead if he doesn't get a prompt response. Make this session lively and fun.

way, snap the lead and bring the dog in, calling the dog at the same time.

The photographs in this chapter should help you envision how this exercise works. Be sure to have a session like this twice a week if you are having problems with "come." Gradually extend the circle physically and psychologically. Broaden the circle so that the full amount of lead length is between each participant. The basic circle should be made up of the dog's immediate family-pack members, but the inclusion of strangers after a few weeks of practice with the regular family can often improve the behavior of aggressive dogs.

HOW YOU CAN USE THIS EXERCISE

Dogs are often so attached to one member of the family that they ignore or refuse to obey others. Regular round-robin sessions will help focus them on other family members. It will also help promote a proper leadership role in each family member. In situations like this, it might be best to exclude the dog's "favorite" from the circle at first. Have that person stay out of sight, thus forcing the dog to relate with other persons who are less desired.

Don't take it personally if the dog doesn't come to you immediately, or if it comes slowly and reluctantly. That is why you have the lead and your voice. *Animate* and encourage the dog, and snap the lead if necessary. *Praise* the dog when the recall is complete. Don't let a session go over ten or twenty minutes, and end it on a playful note. We've seen remarkable improvements in recall and aggression problems, using the round-robin technique twice a week.

Clients usually report great success after a few sessions. Dogs for whom round-robin sessions have been prescribed begin to relate in new ways to family members they had formerly ostracized. After a few initial sessions, many dogs begin to whirl around the circle very quickly, barely stopping for praise from each handler, eager to get to the next. As one client reported after three round-robins with a former fear-biter, "Jake zips around the circle like crazy. He loves it and it's given him a new lease on life. Our family really enjoys it, and we have a waiting list of area kids who want a turn in the circle."

24 One for the Road

Urban dog owners might consider roadworking their dogs as an alternative to daily city strolls. Roadworking is not a matter of hooking up a dog with a rope or chain to a car bumper and then speeding off down the road. There are those who say it is a waste of time and gas, that it does not demand any particular skill, and that it is a drain on the dog. We have never found this to be so here at New Skete and we don't think you will either if you approach roadwork the right way.

Dogs needing weight control and ligament tightening need roadwork. They should be started walking on a fifteen-foot lead, preferably on ploughed ground, dirt, sand, or grass. Do not allow rowdiness in the walking phase. Then phase into jogging, with your dog trotting ahead. Next try a bicycle if you wish, with your dog running alongside. Make sure that you let the dog determine the speed. Never forge out ahead of your dog, and never, never drag the dog. When your walking, jogging, and bicycling are smooth you can begin to work your dog off a car.

When roadworking, always use wide, flat nylon collars. Choose secluded roads with good shoulders. Never work a dog over two miles, no matter what shape the dog is in. City dog owners can roadwork their dogs in local parks or drive out of town to unpopulated areas. Elderly persons who are not physically spry, but who like dogs of the large breeds, can exercise these dogs well with a roadwork program. Keep the leash out from under the car, and do not allow the dog enough leeway to go under a tire.

Make roadwork a highly ritualized and enjoyable event. While roadworking, it is essential to shout en-couragement to your dog *constantly*. It might mean driving every day to an area where you can yell and scream and, in general, make a fool of yourself. We prefer the early morning hours when the pavement is cool, the sun just peeking up, and the air fresh. It is an excellent way for a dog to start the day. Avoid working in the hot sun. If you are able to work close to home, first drive to your starting point with your dog loaded in the car, then begin roadworking, aiming your dog for that highly desirable goal: home, food, water. This will greatly improve the dog's attitude and drive.

BENEFITS OF ROADWORK

Some people think that roadwork is only for show dogs with spongy constitutions who need a crash program of heavy exercise in order to meet a show deadline. We mentioned the benefits of roadwork for the urban pet. But roadwork has many benefits for *all* dogs. Bitches who have recently whelped a litter really profit from this form of exercise. It restores their muscle tone after the strenuous nursing period. Serious obedience fanciers will find roadwork greatly improves trainer–dog relationships and is a welcome break from more precise training routines. Pet owners with hyperactive or seemingly "uncontrollable" canines have much to gain from this form of exercise. The whole roadwork ritual removes both dog and owner from home stresses (telephone, chores, children) and builds good rapport. It vents energy and frustration for the high-energy dog and the high-energy owner. We

Roadworking three dogs out of a station wagon.

Roadworking two dogs off a truck. Notice loose leads.

recommend it as therapy for pet owners with dog management problems. But don't try to handle roadwork alone at first. Get a partner to drive while you control the leash. One last point: besides slimming down a pet, firming up your dog's muscles, or calming down neurotic tendencies, you will be surprised how great these special sessions with your dog make *you* feel!

25 Avoid Canine Incarceration!

If your dog spends any length of time in a play yard, you might be interested in ideas that will help you to make his stay there a pleasure and not an imprisonment. It is amazing how many dog owners have described their dog's "play yard" to us in terms of a gravel enclosure with nothing, absolutely nothing, inside it, except the dog. Boredom and ennui are one of the worst aspects of modern dog life. Chewing, digging, nuisance barking, poor appetites, and stool eating are often in some way connected with boredom. These problems often occur in dogs that have become "kennelized" by such uncreative play yard areas.

Before the professional dog people get up in arms, let us note that we are not against the use of kennels or enclosed areas in dog care. They are necessary. But they can be built with imagination. It doesn't matter whether you have one dog or one hundred, a yard can be well thought out. First, the shape. Rectangular pens encourage dogs to walk and strut about, square kennels encourage dogs to lie down and do nothing. Unfortunately, the rectangular dog run may also encourage fence charging in some dogs, and endless barking, which is correlated with the tension of fence running. If your dog is prone to fence running, change the kennel to a square design and the running will usually stop. For dogs of the large working breeds, we usually suggest square kennels of at least twelve feet by twelve feet, although smaller squares can be used if the dog is not placed in them for too long.

It is important to note that in discussing play area kennels, we refer to the pen in which a dog spends a sizable amount of time, not simply defecation pens. Enclosures constructed solely for defecation can be quite small. More than eight feet in any direction is rarely needed for any dog's elimination needs. We suggest this type of pen so that the owner can effectively clean up after the dog instead of letting the dog squat where it will or eliminate on the curb. Even

A set of tires makes a good obstacle course and helps cut down boredom in the play yard.

A nifty bridge can keep a dog entertained for hours once the dog knows how to use it. Take time to teach the dog.

curbed stools are health hazards, although they beat a mess deposited in the middle of the street, sidewalk, or a neighbor's yard.

Rectangular or square, your kennel should be a fun place. Provide dog-sized toys. Owners of toy breeds might be able to substitute children's toys, but larger breeds need larger toys. You can construct your own, as we often do, with old broom handles, leather scraps, and bells. Just make sure that all sharp edges are sanded down and that no toy is so small that your dog can swallow it. A simple obstacle course of old tires, a curved board cemented at each end for a nifty bridge, and scratch posts can occupy many dogs for hours.* Dogs love any hanging object, especially if

* See "A Puppy Obstacle Course," by Br. Job Evans, *Off Lead* training monthly (May 1977).

it makes some kind of noise. Suspend toys and leather scraps (ask for them at a leather shop) from strong ropes. Always use single strand ropes for hanging toys, and never arrange a hanging toy so low or in such a way that a hanging accident might occur. Rope toys suspended by springs make the toy snap back when the dog lets go, and the dog can play fetch alone. Hanging toys with bells attached keep pets fascinated, but make sure the noise does not bother neighbors. However, most neighbors prefer the sound of bell chimes to incessant barking.

Try to avoid barrier frustration (see Chapter 40 on aggression) by screening the dog's area from busy city street traffic or passersby. If you use cyclone fencing, standard green slats that fit between the chain link are available. Shrubbery can be effectively arranged to block disturbing views that encourage barking and fence running. Within the pen, a ditch or a stone row, or even a row of flowers can often keep the dog away from the fence and in the center of the pen. Gravel is the best all-around footing, but cement and grass may be feasible at times. Cement encourages paw sores and cut pads, so avoid prolonged contact with cement. Grass inevitably wears out, but it is aesthetically pleasing and comfortable for the dog. We find a grass pen with gravel along the sides of the fencing to be the best. The gravel will prevent the grass from being totally destroyed.

Every day introduce a different item into the pen, especially if you leave your dog alone on a daily basis. Favorite toys should always be included, but rotate others to spice up the routine. Rotate water and food in different locations in the pen. When you prune your trees, throw the limbs into the pen for the dog to play with. A large cardboard box enthralls any dog. Sure, the box gets ripped up, and the tree limbs get shredded, and you have to clean up. But it's worth it in the long run. Fresh fruit and vegetables can be used as vitamin-packed toys. Toss a few into the pen every so often. Bones, if offered, should be large *marrow* bones. A dog left alone with a small bone all day can reduce it to such size as to risk lodging it in its mouth or throat. Make sure bones are large and solid, but *not* cooked.

The dog house need not be elaborate but it should provide protection from the elements. In summer, repaint dark-colored houses white to reflect sunlight and heat. The dog should have some options for shade in addition to the house. Trees are best, or a planter of bushes, pruned of their lower branches and with trunks wrapped in tree-tape to prevent the dog from destroying or scratching them.

Finally, do not ignore the possibility of providing your dog with the ultimate diversion and plaything: another dog. Owners with chronic diggers, chewers, barkers, squealers, and house-wreckers have often found that the introduction of a second compatible pet (it can also be a cat!) reduces this behavior. You will have to be sure that the new animal gets off to a right start and does not mimic the bad behavior of the first pet. For dogs who must stay long periods in play yards, a companion can change frustration and boredom to pleasure and play.

Break up monotony whenever and however you can. Use these techniques to eliminate the undesirable forms of pen behavior and encourage proper exercise and play. Give some thought to what your dog does during the day, watch for special interest in toys and devices, and maximize on this interest. A diversified and creative environment is essential, not just for human beings, but for dogs as well.

26 Children and Training

When we counsel dog owners, we usually ask to see the entire family, including the children. Children are usually quite frank about their relationship with the family dog. They will often offer information adults are not aware of or withhold. Perhaps children are more in touch with animals and more aware of the bond that exists between dogs and humans, whereas adults lose track of this knowledge as they grow older. Furthermore, when adult dog owners have fallen out of love with their pet — and have a basically negative attitude toward the dog and training — children often remain positive about the dog and enthusiastic about training. Once they understand training, they can often shed an entirely new light on an otherwise dismal situation. If children love the dog and want to pursue training, they can act as a positive model for their parents. However, prepuberal children cannot always be counted on to train effectively, since their enthusiasm can be short-lived. Adults should work with children when they are actually handling the dog in exercises.

Children in our culture are exposed to a high degree of anthropomorphic conditioning through television and books. They are constantly exposed to animal figures who act like humans. Goofy wears human clothes, drives a car, has a girl friend. Mickey and Minnie Mouse set up housekeeping long ago. Rin-Tin-Tin finds the robbers, saves the family from a burning home, and attacks all the right people. Then there is Lassie. Fairy tales abound with animals that have human traits. Pet-food commercials are filled with animals that talk, dance, and sing, and generally behave like humans. To a child, the dog is a buddy, another child. Children think of dogs as other people.

An excellent book by Maurice Sendak and Matthew Margolis, *Some Swell Pup*, is a children's story that attempts to portray realistically what is involved in purchasing and raising a puppy. This is a good book to read to your children if you plan to purchase a puppy. From early childhood, try to discourage anthropomorphic thinking in your child by providing him or her with realistic stories about dogs and other animals. Have your child go with you to a pound or shelter to expose the child to the variety of breeds — and to the problems of pet population. If there is an obedience class in your area, try to take the child to it and watch together from the sidelines.

We have learned a lot from working with children and dogs, through our kennel boy and girl program, where children come to work with the monastery dogs and puppies and are apprenticed to a monk experienced in child and dog care. We have found that children of all ages have something to give to dogs, from infancy on. An infant, if introduced properly to the dog, can provide the dog with a new sense of responsibility. The toddler can learn to walk the dog under supervision, wash dog dishes, and brush the dog. Older children can feed the dog, take it for walks, help with obedience exercises, and have the dog sleep in their bedroom. Almost all children–canine activities have to be supervised at first. Within every family there are those who have particular talents with animals, and those who don't. Parents should watch for these special abilities and assign dog duties accordingly and not on the basis of sex or age. A sensitivity to animals and a concern for them is more important than sheer efficiency.

Children should be cautioned from the beginning not to come up from behind a dog suddenly. This can have serious consequences no matter how stable the dog is. Dogs generally do not enjoy surprises. Make sure you discuss this with your children. Since children think of dogs as people, training in a class or residential school is often best explained in terms of "school." When we see children here, we talk about the dog's report card and give the dog a diploma. This impresses the children and makes it easier for them to relate to training.

Since consistency is essential in training, you should sit down as a family and discuss training methods *before* getting a dog. If begging by pets is not allowed in your house, the children should understand the necessity of not giving the dog treats. If your dog is to lie down during televi-

Children should not be allowed to run or scream around an untrained and unreliable dog. It can have tragic results.

sion or family recreation, all family members should realize this and enforce it. If necessary, type out the rules and post them where all can refer to them.

Children often become hysterical when a dog must be restrained or disciplined, creating more havoc than the original incident. If the children already understand the role of discipline, chaotic scenes can be avoided. Parents should explain from an early age that dogs are not children. Children should not be allowed to scream around the pet; it can result in aggressive incidents. Tug-o-war games, sexual stimulation of the dog, or "siccing" the dog on others should be taboo. In some very young children some tail-yanking, ear-pulling, and rough handling is inevitable. When you go to buy a puppy, ask whether the puppies have been exposed to children. Remember that the outgoing, fire-brand type of pup is not necessarily the best for an active family. Trust a behaviorally oriented breeder who has worked with families to help you select the right pup.

Once a family of six visited New Skete. They were interested in a German shepherd and admired the breed, but they were concerned over incidents they had heard concerning children and shepherds. We were surrounded by several grown dogs that we were evaluating together. The father of the family asked the monk who was showing them the dogs, "What is the point of a good breeding program?" At this point, a three-year-old toddler waddled over to one of the shepherds, grasped its tail, and gave it a good jerk. The surprised dog

Swimming together is an activity dogs and children can enjoy immensely.

moved a few inches, turned, and licked the child's face. The monk turned to the father of the family. "That," he said, "is the point of a good breeding program."

Many a mother winds up with the task of feeding, caring for, and walking a pet that is supposedly the responsibility of another member of the family. It's no surprise that much of the pet advice in our culture is dished out in women's magazines. Women get stuck with the kids in our culture, and they also get the dogs in the bargain. A wise mother will anticipate this and avoid allowing a dog into the family unless she is confident that the responsible individual will care for it, or, if she is actually to be the one caring for it, that she has the time for the pet.

Keeping children and strange dogs apart is the best preventative for avoiding tragic biting incidents. Caution your children not to approach strange dogs unless you are there, even if encouraged to do so by others. Many dogs fear children and vice versa, and the resulting conflicts can result in permanent damage. Dogs trained in guard work learn to attack an upraised hand, so caution your children to stand still and walk away slowly if menaced by a strange dog. Above all, they should not scream or run away. This will encourage the dog to attack. If you know of an unfriendly dog in your neighborhood, notify the owners — don't wait for an unfortunate incident to occur.

Starting Off Right

27 Puppy Training

A client came to us with a six-month-old Siberian husky female who had just destroyed an expensive Persian rug, eaten three Dinah Shore record albums, and excavated the entire backyard. The dog had practically pulled the owner's arms out of their sockets by furious leash-lunging. The client asked if this was a good time to start training. Our answer was that it was a good time to *continue* training. We asked what kind of training had been done to date. "Well, I've taught her to sit for a treat," the client proudly announced. Anything else? "Well, no. Can you really expect anything else? Some books I read said not to train before the dog is six months old, and my friends said the same thing. So I just house-trained her. Frankly, I thought I was bringing her in for training a little early! But she's smart enough, don't you think?"

This client was confused as to when puppy training should begin. She had been indoctrinated with the myth that dog training cannot commence until the dog is past the sixth month. But the dog was driving her crazy and she decided to bring her for training when she turned six months. As she noted, correctly in this case, the dog was intelligent. Indeed, most puppies are intelligent and willing to learn, if taught correctly. Training can begin as early as the *third week* of a puppy's life. This chapter will help you to teach your puppy standard exercises and to expose your pup to a broad range of experiences that will deepen your relationship while the puppy is still growing.

Kindergarten Puppy Training, or KPT as it is called, began years ago when trainers like the Pearsalls recognized its worth and started holding KPT classes. We owe these early KPT trainers a great debt for helping to educate the public to the possibilities of puppy training. Researchers like Dr. J. P. Scott and Dr. J. L. Fuller had laid the groundwork for KPT by demonstrating in laboratory studies the full range of puppy learning ability. Clarence Pfaffenberger and Dr. Michael Fox later amplified these findings.

Many breeders socialize and train their own stock at a young age and encourage their clients to do so, yet the "you-can't-train-a-dog-before-six-months" myth is still strong. It is true that regular leash training as described in many training books can be harmful to a young puppy. The leash correction can be too sharp and possibly traumatic for the pup. A pup's skeletal structure is not fully set until it is six months old, and jerk-and-pull corrections can be harmful.* But other, less manipulative training techniques are highly effective in training puppies. Formal obedience training after six months will be more difficult for the dog that has not had training earlier.

If there is a KPT class in your area, do enroll in it. The class will probably

---

* See William E. Campbell, *Behavior Problems in Dogs* (Santa Barbara, Calif.: American Veterinary Publications, 1975), p. 149.

meet on a weekly basis and include between five and twenty puppies and owners. If you can't find such a class, follow the instructions here until the time you can enroll your dog in advanced training instruction.

Before you jump into training your puppy, it is a good idea to understand what happens to puppies physically and psychologically as they grow. For the first seven weeks the puppy has a special need for its littermates. If you are buying a puppy, you can feel free to take one home when it is between seven and ten weeks old, but not earlier. After ten weeks, make sure the puppy has been socialized at the kennel. Between approximately eight and ten weeks, a puppy passes through what specialists call "the fear period." During this time, the puppy is especially susceptible to stress and poor handling. Each puppy experiences this in a different way. It is important to be aware of the fear period, but don't make the puppy live in a cocoon during this or any other period of its early life. Social isolation will destroy a puppy faster than any of the most inhumane training methods.

Training the puppy to follow, walk on a leash, sit, lie down, and chew only on acceptable objects is perfectly fine during this period, but make sure only capable persons work with the pup. For instance, if the pup is brought home during this time, don't allow children who are rough with the dog to handle it until it is ten weeks old. Some children simply do not have the knack of puppy socializing and training and must wait until the puppy is more mature. If your pup is oversensitive to the leash, postpone leash work until the eleventh week.

One cardinal rule of puppy training: *never lose your temper.* These exercises are meant to be fun for both you and your puppy.*

NAMING THE PUP

In general we try to name our pups using short, two-syllable names. Names that end on soft "a" or hard "o" are excellent (Sarah, Bosco, Sandra, Laika, Elko, and so forth). While there is nothing wrong with the traditional "Spot," we have had quicker response from puppies with two-syllable names. Do not use names that rhyme with or sound like obedience commands. Remember that "cute" names may sound quaint on puppies (Cupcake, Huggy, Baby, and the like) but lose their charm when the dog is older. Joke names or names that emphasize a physical characteristic of the breed or individual dog are a matter of personal taste. We know some city dwellers who have deliberately named their dogs with "rough-type" names in order to increase their protection value (Blacktooth, Ripper, Lance, and Terror are some we've heard). Again, you have to live with your dog's name.

Once you know your dog, you can even change it. We know two shepherd owners who own two dogs with the innocent names of Dagmar and Cain — not exactly terrifying call names. The dogs themselves are mild-mannered and easygoing. But when suspicious-looking persons are seen

* Our thanks to Mrs. Joyce Arner, whose puppy class outline helped us to shape this chapter.

Call the puppy between two handlers. Open your arms wide and kneel down.

around the home, the owners call the dogs by shouting, "Killer and Fang, come here quickly!" It has proven to be very effective.

Your main concern should be to choose a name that the dog can hear with ease and understand, one that complements the dog's personality.

COMING WHEN CALLED

First, the pup must learn its name. Say it often, especially when you catch the pup looking at you. Begin some practice with two handlers. Call the pup back and forth between handlers. At first, leave only about five or six feet between the two handlers. Lengthen this space as the pup progresses.

Call the puppy in a happy tone of voice, and when the puppy comes to you, praise it exuberantly. You should be on your knees when you call the pup. Your arms should be open wide, to help "funnel" the pup into you. If your pup does not wag its tail and have a happy look in its eye when it is coming to you, perhaps you didn't have enough "bubbles" when you called its name. Don't take it personally if a pup is slow coming to you. Continue calling the puppy, and give it encouragement the minute it starts to move toward you. Keep calling if the pup doesn't come. It may be confused. Pat the ground hard, click your fingers, clap your hands, or jingle a set of keys. When the pup comes to you, praise it physically and verbally. Face the puppy toward the other handler when it is being called back.

If your pup is coming pertly between two handlers, you can go to circle-come work. Add another handler, and space yourselves about five feet apart. Attach a light lead to the pup's collar, have your partner call the pup, then toss the end of the leash to your partner. If the pup does not come quickly, have your partner give the leash a tug and if necessary bring the pup all the way in. Have the pup sit in front of you when it comes. Some pups may jump up and paw each handler. Do not discipline this, but gently ease the puppy to a sitting position, and continue praising it. Remember, no punishment should ever be connected with the action of coming. Continue having the puppy called around the circle. Puppy call-in sessions should last five or ten minutes each until the pup is five months old. After that, fifteen minutes a session is fine. End your call-in sessions with a play session. Leave the leash on during the play period. This helps the pup feel comfortable with the leash on and associate wearing it with pleasant experiences, not just "work."

When you call your pup, use the dog's name and the word "come." Do not use more than one name, and do not use affectionate nicknames here. Remember, the more you work on a prompt recall in your dog's early days, the fewer recall problems you will have later on. Almost every dog has on occasion failed to come when called, but puppies who have experienced coming when called as a happy experience early in life will tend to have a better attitude toward the recall later.

FOLLOWING

Once a day, for ten to twenty minutes, have an off-lead follow session with your pup.* Take the pup alone to an area where there are few distractions. Set the pup down and slowly walk away, keeping the pup's attention by talking in an encouraging, animated tone. Say the pup's name frequently. Stop every so often, crouch down, and praise the pup. Then rise and begin walking again. Make plenty of turns in your follow session. Trace a figure-eight every so often. Most puppies, from

* See William E. Campbell, op. cit., p. 149.

As the pup progresses, switch to circle work. Use a leash to help guide the puppy to you.

After the puppy comes to you, throw the leash to the next person before he calls the puppy in.

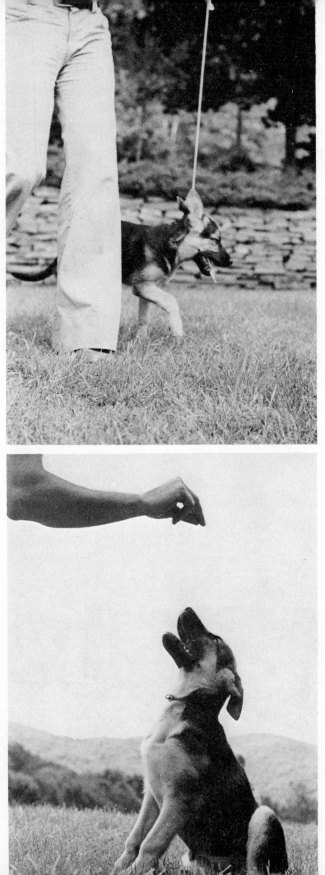

*Keep the leash up high
in early leash training.*

*Puppies should be
taught to sit by using a
nonphysical technique.
Hold one hand above
the pup's head, give
praise when the pup
sits.*

the fourth week on, naturally follow a moving human being in much the same way they tag along with their mother. Often no coaxing is necessary and the puppy may even be underfoot. This is fine — the point is to keep the pup with you, as near as possible, by any method except by treating with food. You may want to use a set of keys, a squeak toy, or a whistle to help orient the pup to you.

While this session might become boring in time and seem uneventful, keep it up for at least three weeks after you receive your new pup. This will aid your rapport in several ways. It helps the pup recognize you as leader, the one to follow. If the pup is comfortable and happy when following you, it will help to eliminate recall problems in the coming months when your puppy will enter a more independent stage and be more easily attracted away from you.

LEASH WORK

Leash work can begin as early as six or seven weeks of age. The revealing term "leash-breaking," often used by trainers to explain how a puppy should be introduced to the leash, is unfortunate, since there should be no "breaking" of the pup involved. If you practice the following exercises, leash work will follow more easily. First, accustom your pup to wearing a collar. Use a flat leather buckle collar if possible. As you hold the pup in your arms, put the collar on snug once or twice a day, to get the pup used to the feel of the collar on its neck. Then begin by attaching a light leash to the pup's collar and letting

the pup drag it along on a normal follow session. Don't use heavy metal leashes on puppies. After the dragging phase, the trick is to get the leash on and begin walking without the pup's knowing the leash is on. As you pet the pup, snap on your lead. As you begin to walk, hold the lead almost straight up, out of the pup's way, and don't apply any pressure to the lead. At some point, the pup will stop, and feel the lead. Don't pull the pup along just yet. Stop, bend over, and say, "Okay, Spot, let's go!" Use the same animated tone of voice you used in your follow sessions. If the pup balks, stop for a minute and reassure the pet. Some pups brace themselves dramatically and become quite vocal. These are usually pups that have had trouble sticking close on the follow exercises. You will need to pull the pup gently and with encouragement until it decides to come along. Some researchers have found that males tend to be more feisty on initial leash work, running ahead and vocalizing when they hit the end of the leash.* Whatever the reaction, get the pup focused on you and begin again. Make your first sessions short and try to end on a happy note. Leave the leash on and have a play session with the puppy.

TEACHING THE SIT

Puppies should be taught to sit using a nonphysical technique. One hand is held above the pup's head, finger tips closed together, two feet above the pup's eyes. As the pup looks up at

* See Dr. J. L. Fuller, *Hereditary Differences in Trainability* (Roscoe B. Jackson Memorial Laboratory, Bar Harbor, Maine).

your hand, and begins to sink in the rear, give the command "Sit." After the command, even as the dog begins to sit, praise the dog until it is fully seated. Repeat if the pup does not sit the first time. If the puppy is simply looking up and not sitting, repeat, and with your other hand, lean over and give the pup's rump a light tap. We have found this method of teaching the sit is faster than harsher leash and training-collar methods. Do not use treats to train the sit. After the puppy sits, hold it in place as you praise it.

TEACHING THE DOWN

Like the puppy sit, the puppy down is best taught with a minimum of manipulation. Use a ball or other toy to aid in teaching the down. First, sit the pup. It is easier for a dog to lie down from the sitting position than from the standing. Show the pup the toy, and as the pup focuses on it, lower it directly to the ground about six inches in front of the pup's feet. As you do this give the command "Down." As the pup lowers its head to play with the ball, begin gently praising the pup, repeating "Down" if necessary. Later, after your pup is going down, use your empty hand instead of a toy, your fingers clenched together in a suggestive way. Some pups may need a little pressure on their shoulders as you give the command. The physical methods described for older dogs in this book might not be right for puppies, as they involve a lot of body contact. Never try to train a puppy to lie down using the "pulley" method of

stepping on the leash and forcing the dog down. Most puppies respond well to the nonphysical method. Do not use treats to train the down.

In training the sit and down, make sure you limit puppy sit and down sessions to five or six commands at a time. One session in the morning and one in the evening is sufficient.

TETHERING THE PUP AT NIGHT

The best place for a puppy to sleep is on the floor at the foot of your bed. Avoid socially isolating the puppy at night. For the first few nights, an inverted cardboard box with a large hole cut out makes a good denlike resting place. A wind-up alarm clock can help keep the pup calm the first night, as it approximates the mother's heartbeat and comforts the pup. Some owners might prefer to tether their pup for the night. This can help prevent overnight accidents (since most puppies will not soil their immediate area) and help curb destructive chewing. The tether can be quite short at first, a foot or two will do. Use a metal tether. The puppy will snack on any other material and eventually free itself, possibly in the middle of the night. The pup will probably fight the tether the first night. Reassure it without coddling. You might try attaching the pup before you are actually ready to retire and let the pup fight the tether while you read. Above all, don't give in and release the pup. Some initial whining and protest is inevitable.

Attach the end of the tether to a

Lower your hand to the ground to teach the puppy the down.

The pup will follow your hand down; as it does, say the word "down," and praise it.

strong, immovable object, such as a furniture leg or the bed itself. Make sure that the tether cannot break, and that it is not attached to an object that can be pulled away by the pup. Puppies are strong little critters when they want to be. One man attached his puppy to a hamper on wheels and retired for the night. About three in the morning the puppy pulled the hamper to the top of the stairs and sent the hamper and itself crashing to the bottom. We heard about the incident when the owner later brought the puppy to us to teach it to climb stairs, a skill it had not yet acquired. A little research pinpointed why the dog had such an aversion to stairs.

In general, our practice is to keep our pups tethered at night until two objectives are accomplished. First, the pup must be fully housebroken. Second, all chewing, digging, and other puppy mischief must have ceased. Only then do we allow the pup freedom in our bedroom at night.

BEHAVIOR AT NIGHT

Since our bedroom section is in the cloister, and silence is enforced, no puppy yodeling or barking is allowed. If you want a puppy that "alarm barks" you can allow some barking at night. However, shush it after a few seconds, or the pup will go overboard. Chapter 18, "Where Is Your Dog This Evening?" describes "bedroom etiquette" for adult canines and applies to puppies as well, but there are some exceptions. If your pup pipes up during the night, it could be telling you it needs to go out. Young puppies

that are not fully housebroken will need a trip out approximately every four hours. As the pup matures, after twelve weeks of age, it should be able to pass a night of eight hours duration without needing to go out, assuming it has not been fed immediately prior to bedtime. Many a pup owner gets into the "three-A.M.-trip-out ritual" needlessly. The pup whines, the owner gets up and takes the pup out. But if you have previously let the pup out and are sure it is "empty" or relatively so, shush the pup with a sharp, "No, go back to sleep." Don't become a doorman for the pup. At some point, the pup must learn control.

When you tether or crate your pup for the night, provide it with some toys and chewables. Remove food and water. If you are housebreaking the pup, remove water at least four hours prior to retiring, and feed the puppy its second or third meal early in the afternoon. This early feeding will give the pup time to eliminate before settling down for the night.

USING A DOG CRATE

A dog crate can be used to help you train your puppy in a variety of ways. Dogs are basically den animals, and a crate approximates the den of their wolf ancestors. Crates are not cruel or inhumane, as long as they have ample room and are not used as punishment. The open-air crate is best. Metal crates are a must. Wooden ones eventually get chewed. The open-air crate seems to help some dogs accept confinement more easily, and can be covered with a blanket if need be. If your puppy barks in the crate, go to the crate, clap your hands, and tell the pup, "*No, no barking.*" If the pup continues, add a physical correction by pinching the pup's mouth shut or tapping it on the nose.

You can use the crate at night or during periods of time when you will be gone for a few hours. Since most dogs are fastidious about their immediate area, you can use the crate to help the pup spend time alone without relieving itself. The crate is a temporary solution until the dog is housebroken and can be trusted alone in the house while you are sleeping or gone.

Later, you will find other uses for the crate. Many dogs prefer to ride in a crate in the car. When you are moving or carrying a large amount of baggage, a crate can save valuable space. If you plan to travel with your dog, it is wise to crate-condition the dog in advance. When we raise litters, we let the pups use an open crate as a play house, as some pups might eventually use a crate in their new homes. Never ship a dog in a shipping crate on a train or plane unless you have first conditioned the dog to the crate. If you do need to ship, use the smallest crate possible. If the crate is too large, the dog will be bounced around in transit. With a small crate, the animal can brace itself against the walls.

Crate-condition for travel or for home by putting the pup in the crate for ten minutes. Gradually increase this period of time, on a day-to-day basis. Many owners take the precaution of removing their dog's collar during the time it is in the crate, to prevent it from being caught.

ASKING TO GO OUT

Our procedures for house-training puppies can be found in Chapter 36 on house-training. Asking to go out is best taught in puppyhood and is a service any canine owner appreciates. If you want a puppy that asks to go out, begin early by recognizing the signs the puppy gives indicating it wants to go out to eliminate. Some pups will bark or whine. Be sure to respond by opening the door. Condition the pup that does not indicate vocally a desire to go out by first reading the other signs that elimination is forthcoming. Some pups will pace, noses to the ground. Others may go to the door and scratch it. Still others may come to you and jump up. Whatever the sign, read it quickly and take the pup to the door, asking in an excited tone of voice, "Do you want to go out?" Make sure you use the same phrase and the same door each time you let the pup out. If the pup lives in a family, everyone should be consistent about what phrase is used when inviting the pup out for elimination. But don't let the pup out each time it nears a door. Pups do not need out every hour on the hour, and you should be careful to avoid the extreme of becoming a doorman for the pup.

While asking to go out is a convenience, don't let the pup overdo it. If you are in the middle of preparing a meal or in some other situation where you cannot immediately let the dog out, say "No, wait!" and let the pup out as soon as you can. At night, follow the instructions for silencing whiners mentioned earlier. If your pup does have an accident, follow the procedures outlined in the house-training section. Clean up the area with disinfectant, but apply a final solution of white vinegar and water. This will cancel out the odor from the dog's point of view.

SUBMISSIVE URINATION

Submissive urination is distinguished from house-soiling because it is involuntary and usually takes place when the puppy is in a subordinate position and releases a puddle, or possibly a flood, of urine. The puppy does not mean to urinate but to show submission. Though the behavior invariably stops with time, here are some techniques to help you through the period if you experience this problem.

Above all, don't punish the puppy. Try not to tower over the pup in a threatening manner. Crouch down when you call the pup, and praise it by stroking it under the chin and on the shoulder region. Experience will teach you what times your puppy tends to urinate involuntarily. Greetings and departures, visits of company and relatives, or wild activity by children often triggers submissive urination. Don't isolate the pup from these situations, but try to delay the submissive response by backing away and calling the pup to you. Try to keep active children away from the pup, but invite gentler children to play with it. Puppies that wet submissively for adults often will not do so for children, so if you can find a placid child willing to take the pup for walks and socialize it, this may be helpful. Keep your greetings low-key.

Gradually build the pup's confidence by taking it for walks on busy streets and in other people-congested areas. Avoid all spanking and punishment for submissive urination.

DISCIPLINE FOR PUPPIES

In general, puppies do not often need harsh physical correction. Some situations merit discipline, and we suggest that you use the shakedown method, which is described in Chapter 10. KPT is designed to eliminate the necessity of dishing out physical punishment later on in life. But every dog occasionally gets out of line, and you should not hesitate to use physical correction for big offenses, such as overbarking, biting, or house-soiling. Different breeds need different approaches. German shepherds, Dobermans, and Rottweilers can often get themselves into situations in which physical discipline is merited. Terriers can be highly kinetic and often need sustained eye contact and only occasionally physical discipline. You must "read" your own dog.

PUPPY CHEWING

Almost every puppy, at some point, chews something it is not supposed to chew. It might be an old shoe or it might be a precious family heirloom, if you are naïve enough to leave one within reach. Before you bring your puppy home, "chew-proof" your home as much as possible. Make careful arrangements for shoes and socks to be up off the floor, throw rugs stapled down, and valuable objects put away, at least until the puppy is

Taking an object out of the pup's mouth.

over its chewing stage. Provide your pup with a blanket or dog bed where it can go when tired, preferably in your own bedroom. In this area, provide the pup with a rawhide or nylon bone. Meat-scented bones are excellent. Do not use real bones. Stay away from cute toys sold at pet stores, or contraptions that can be broken or chewed apart. Make this bone the center of attention for the pup by playing fetch with it, wiggling it on the floor and letting the pup chase it, and giving it to the pup whenever it begins to nibble on any forbidden object. This is *the* toy. Get a few different sizes of play bones so that you can graduate the size as the pup grows older. Before leaving the pup, whether confined in a crate, tethered, or left outside, roll this bone between your palms for a couple of minutes to leave your scent on it, and dramatically present it to the pup as you leave home. Another method of orienting the pup to the bone is to rub your saliva on it. If you plan to take your pup for a ride in the car and leave it there, take the special bone along too, and present it to the pup as you leave the car.

Whenever you catch the pup chewing on something forbidden, say "No!" strongly, and immediately take the object out of the pup's mouth or remove the pup from the scene. Immediately get the play bone and present it to the pup, saying, "Here, *this* is for you, this is your toy." Avoid punishing the pup or trying to tear forbidden chewables out of its mouth. *Never* play tug-o-war with a puppy, whether in jest or by accident, as often happens when owners try to take something out of a pup's mouth. To get an object out of a pup's mouth, open the jaws by placing your hand across the top of the muzzle behind the teeth, thumb on one side and fingers on the other, and with the other hand pull down the bottom jaw. As the pup drops the object, say "Good!"

One common response to a chewing problem is to provide the pup with myriad chew toys, in the hopes that the pup will find this vast array satisfying and stay clear of taboo objects. While somewhat logical from a human point of view, this technique usually backfires since it conditions the pup to perceive practically everything as a potential chew toy. Provide one or two toys and stop there. If you must have several toys for several locations (car, bedroom, basement), make them all the same kind of toy.

Remember, the pup *needs* to chew. Never completely forbid your pup to chew. This is unnatural and ill-advised. The pup's proper oral development will be stunted, and since the pup was never allowed to chew on anything and go through the normal teething stage, it may decide to postpone oral activity until later on. The renewed activity could include destructive chewing of objects and possibly humans. Focus your pup on the proper chew articles, but don't deprive it of chewing completely. This stage can last as long as eight months, or as short as four months, depending on the individual dog.

PRAISING YOUR PUPPY

Physical and verbal praise are important for puppies. Include a play session with both of you on all fours, at least twice a week. Keep the pup animated and happy during formal obedience work. However, the tendency to coddle the pup must be avoided. An overindulged pup is soon spoiled and takes advantage of the rest of the family-pack by assuming a leadership role. We have seen puppies who are dictators. When they whine, they are picked up. If they scratch a door, they are immediately let out. If they bark at someone, the owner pets them and thanks them. If they bite someone, they may or may not be scolded, depending on what the owner thinks of the victim. If the puppy wants praise, it need only nudge or jump up on the owner and it is immediately given. If the owner responds to such behavior by coddling and cuddling the pup, the pup soon learns that such behavior elicits affection. It learns to turn on this behavior whenever it wants attention, which may be every other minute.

A more responsible approach to

praising your puppy includes praising the pup for good behavior and avoiding the temptation to praise the pup simply because it is there. While affectionate petting and squeezing are a part of any initial puppy–owner relationship, decrease this behavior as the puppy matures and begins training. Praise the pup when it fulfills a command, like sit or come. It only takes a second to ask the pup to sit before praising it, and it will be well worth your while, for it orients the pup to obedience early in life. Be sure to include fetch and play sessions in your puppy's life. Don't impose a Spartan regime on the dog, but make praise meaningful.

LONELY PUPPIES

Patience and a sincere desire for constant companionship are the two most important traits necessary to raise a healthy, happy puppy. If you are the kind of person who needs long periods of time completely alone, or who feels occasionally claustrophobic if anyone is around, don't get a dog. A dog will always be there, asking for attention and directions, asking to serve. If this gets on your nerves, reconsider whether you want a puppy. There is nothing wrong with admitting that cats are your type of pet, or that a bowl of goldfish would adapt better to your style. Respect for living things requires an appreciation for their innate needs and desires and the ability to fulfill these, at least to some degree.

A belated realization of the above sometimes leads to puppies with behavior problems. Puppies can be bored, neglected, in a word, lonely. Puppies simply cannot endure long periods of isolation. They are pack animals, born and raised in a litter. They need social experience throughout puppyhood and later life. Lonely puppies are puppies that are left alone while their owners work. They are pups who are refused admission to the bedroom for sleeping and banished to the kitchen or basement (often on the pretext that they must "protect" the house — something they will never feel compelled to do unless they are first endeared to the masters of the house). Lonely puppies often lack play experience with humans or other dogs. Instead, they are continually stroked, cuddled in the owner's arms. It is quite possible to be lonely but touched all day. The best food, trinkets, treats, and even professional training does not matter if the puppy lives a hermit's life.

Lonely puppies vent their frustrations by chewing, digging, barking, whining, and by scratching doors and walls. They crave human contact and seek to escape from their isolation, even though they may appear shy or aggressive around humans at first. If you follow the directives in this chapter, your puppy should not be lonely, by your standards or his. If, however, you decide to modify the pup's life-style after deciding that the pup can "take it," and isolate the pup for significant periods of time, you will most probably wind up with behavioral problems.

What it all adds up to is this: don't get a pup unless you have plenty of time to spend with it. Don't expect a dog to be a cat or a hamster. Answer the following questions honestly if you are planning to get a puppy. If you already have a dog, these questions might serve as a helpful review of your responsibilities as a dog owner.*

Will someone be home to provide meals for the animal according to a fixed schedule?

Will someone be home during the day to look after the dog?

If you're considering a puppy, are you willing to exercise the puppy at least twice a day, according to a set schedule?

Are you willing to secure proper obedience training for the dog?

Are you willing to pay for all inoculations, periodic veterinary exams, and any emergency treatment the dog may need?

Are you willing to pay the cost of spaying or neutering your pet to prevent the birth of more unwanted puppies in a nation already saturated with pets?

Are you willing to obey the leash laws of your community?

Are you committed to caring for the dog for its lifetime?

We feel we should end this chapter on a serious note, since getting a puppy is a serious matter, even though the experience has joyful aspects.

* The above questions are taken from "A Checklist for Potential Pet Owners," The Humane Society of the United States, 2100 L Street, N.W., Washington, D.C. 20037.

Standard Obedience Exercises

28 Starting Out

The following chapters will help you to teach your dog how to heel, sit, sit and stay, lie down, lie down and stay, and come when called. The most popular exercises will be the last two. Most dog owners will be happy if Fido simply lies down or comes when he is called. But in order to teach these two exercises effectively, your dog must know something about the others. As we will explain in the following chapters, the other exercises are not strictly ornamental — they can be used to great advantage. We will try to explain fully what each exercise entails. We will try also to demonstrate at least two methods of teaching each exercise. We realize each dog is an individual and not every dog responds well to every method. Finally, we will try to include examples in each chapter of how the exercise can be used practically in your day-to-day life with your pet.

The emphasis is on the practical application of each exercise, and not on "showing off" your dog to strangers or on parlor tricks, like shaking hands, "praying," rolling over, and the like. These tricks may be entertaining, but the dog who can shake hands, roll over, and pray but cannot lie down and who runs away when called can be a problem to its owner.

Nor is our emphasis on training for the professional obedience ring or for competition. While what we say does not contradict training methods for the ring, this book is geared to help

you to read your dog and thereby deepen your relationship with your dog. If you are interested in showing your dog in the obedience ring, you may want to consult some of the many books that concentrate on that field, listed at the back of this book. Nevertheless, even those who show their dogs professionally need to stop occasionally and reevaluate their relationship with their dogs. Regardless of how well a dog knows its exercises, the total relationship between dog and master remains the most important aspect of having a dog as a companion.

Here's a story that illustrates what we mean. A famous dog, well known for his high scores in the obedience ring, arrived at the show grounds. As we watched, the owner carefully opened the dog's metal crate, warning the dog not to barge out. Instead, the dog nudged open the door of the crate, practically knocking over his owner as he barreled out of the station wagon. Luckily, the owner had left the dog's leash on and pinned it with his foot, thereby preventing the dog's escape. He immediately snapped the dog to a heel position and began drilling the dog in the obedience exercises. The dog responded like a robot. He racked up a high score in the ring. Immediately after the long down, which is taken in a group with other dogs, the owner leashed his dog and heeled him out of the ring. But once outside the ring rope, the dog lunged ahead, practically dragging his trainer across an empty field, back to the station wagon. The dog leaped into the crate in the car, and the trainer, exhausted after the "ride," slammed the crate door shut. While the dog performed well, one wonders what the total dog–human relationship was like.

This story is not typical of many dogs shown in the obedience ring, but it does illustrate a major pitfall in training obedience exercises. And that is: don't make your dog into a robot! Obedience training does not turn a dog into a zombie, but a bad trainer does. Train with spirit, humor, and most of all, physical and verbal *praise!*

29 Equipment

What kind of equipment do you need to train your dog? First, you will need a good-quality leather or cotton webbed six-foot leash. You will need a training collar of steel or nylon. If it is of steel, it should have links that are pounded *flat*, not rounded, so that the collar will have good, clean action when pulled and not hurt the dog or snag on itself because of faulty construction. You may also need a long twenty- or thirty-foot rope leash. You can make one easily by attaching a length of rope to your six-foot training lead. Do not invest money in fancy harness contraptions or prong collars. (Yes, we know they are sometimes advocated, but frankly we have never seen a dog that really needs one.) The training collar should *fit the dog!* The most common error clients make in "outfitting" their dog for training is to purchase a training collar that is many times too large. *Measure* your dog's neck. Training collars are usually sold in even-inch

models, so select one that allows three or four inches of slack when it is pulled tight on the dog. This means the training collar will be snug going over the dog's ears when you put it on. The larger your training collar, the longer it takes for your correctional tug to be telegraphed to your dog when you use the training leash for a correction. You owe it to the dog to make your corrections immediately and you can't do it with oversize equipment.

There is a definite, right way to put the training collar on. Stand on the left side of your dog. Put the collar on so that the end of the collar that has the ring comes *over* the dog's neck and through the inactive ring. Pull the collar. It should loosen up when you release the ring, but if you have the collar on wrong, it will flop over and hang from the inactive loop. The photographs in this chapter should help you in outfitting your dog.

Training collars should be steel and have pounded, flat links.

A good lead has no sewn parts that can break. Note braided construction on this lead. You will need a six-foot lead.

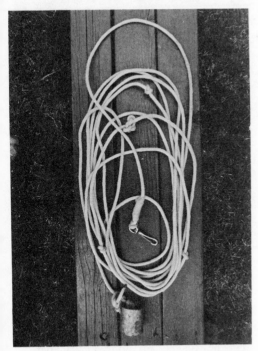

You can adapt a long nylon rope for recall work quite easily. Put a weight on one end. Wear gloves to prevent rope burn.

We feel strongly that a dog should wear a training collar all the time. Some feel that the dog risks getting hung up on tree limbs or furniture and possibly choking accidentally. This is a point, but we've found that the advantages of wearing the collar all the time outweigh the possible accidents that could occur. Once the training collar is on, it can serve as a "mini-leash" when the handler simply inserts a finger in the active ring.

The long leash will aid you in teaching your dog to come when called. Nylon rope is a good choice but wear gloves to prevent your hands from being burned if the rope is pulled through fast. Stay away from twine or string. It can break or

The correct way to put on the training collar.

cut your hands if the dog pulls away quickly.

If you want to find good-quality dog-training equipment, call an obedience instructor or an obedience school. Don't count on items pur-chased in supermarkets to last. As the pet market continues to boom, there will be plenty of poor-quality pet equipment available. Remember, a training collar that breaks in the middle of a training session can cost you valuable training time. A defective leash that snaps when your dog bolts at a cat on a busy city street can possibly cost the dog its life. Get good, top-quality equipment.

30 Heeling

The object of the heel and the automatic sit is to train your dog to walk at your left side without pulling ahead or lagging behind – and to glide into a sit when you stop. Heeling is a practical, useful skill. It is not an ornamental part of dog training, reserved for professional trainers. The heel is the first lesson your dog will learn, and in many ways the heel and the way you teach it may be instrumental in changing the way you and your dog relate to one another. This exercise is important in reordering faulty dog–owner relationships where the animal perceives itself as the leader and, most probably, takes the *owner* for a walk every day. If your dog fits this description, and if your arms are continually being popped out of their sockets by a lunging beast, you will appreciate the necessity of this exercise.

Trainers disagree on how the heel should be taught. We try to view this exercise as part of the overall relationship between dog and owner, and not as a punitive measure or, on the other hand, a frill. We feel the heel should be approached in a firm way. You should steel yourself for some rough action. Determine from the beginning that you are going to learn to work as a team with your dog and will eventually be able to walk smoothly together. Don't go into the exercise saying "My dog can't heel." In our experience, we have never met a dog that cannot heel.

To begin heeling work, select an area that has good footing and that is large enough to permit walking in any direction. (Don't try to train your dog to heel when you are wearing sandals and walking on grass!) The area should be quiet – while distractions are important in training, your first heeling lesson is no time for them; make sure there will be no distractions or interruptions. With training collar on correctly, leash in your right hand, your dog on your left side, step forward with your left foot, the foot closest to the dog, jutting it out demonstratively. At the same time give your dog the command, "Duke, *heel.*" Prefix the word "heel" with the dog's name, but emphasize the command. As you move out, your dog may or may not follow you. Give a smart snap on the lead if the dog decides to stay put. If the dog follows,

Start with the dog on your left. Get the dog's attention by making eye contact and praising it.

When you start out, jutt your left foot forward dramatically. Make sure the dog sees you start out and hears you give the command "Heel."

walk along, encouraging the dog with the command *heel*, slapping your left thigh with your free hand. You will have to grasp the leash with your right hand to do this. And we mean *slap* your left thigh. The dog must be able to hear the orienting sound for it to be helpful. If your thigh is red after the session, good; chances are your dog heard and understood the signal. Don't be afraid to exaggerate commands and movements during this initial session. Your dog must hear the word "heel" to learn it. While you don't have to scream the command, you must pronounce it clearly. Don't baby-talk it. Make it audible. During this initial session, your serious tone of voice is important. It should be loud, clear, firm.

There are any number of moves your dog can attempt while you are heeling. Literally anything is possible. Since so many dogs are not properly leash-trained as pups and never restrained in any way early in life, many have an initial abhorrence of a leash. To some dogs, it is a tether that is meant to be chewed and broken; to others, it is a signal to run to a corner, curl up, and die. Other dogs might respond by attempting to melt into the ground, or by scaling the handler's back and sides. A Labrador retriever we had for training climbed up the training-Brother's back, perched himself on the Brother's shoulders for a frenzied moment, and then hurled himself to the ground.

Your dog's reaction will probably not be so extreme. Whatever the response, you can correct it if you know how to use the training collar properly while heeling. The training collar should be snapped, smartly and firmly, when you correct lunging ahead or lagging. Don't haul the dog behind you like a trailer. If your dog decides to go into the "mule act" of simply not moving at all, stop, return to the dog, make eye contact, and firmly announce, "Okay, Duke, you're coming with *me*, now *heel*," emphasizing the command word. Then, as you take off, pop the lead firmly. Your training collar snaps should be felt by the dog. Make your corrections fast and *release* the pressure of the collar immediately. Don't hang or haul the dog, and don't apply continual pressure on the training collar. Those methods just don't work. The "pop-snap" type of training-collar correction does. It helps to orient the dog and serves as a directional signal that is convincing.

Don and Joyce Arner, trainers in upstate New York, have a good idea for teaching training-collar technique. They suggest that their students practice by attaching their training collar to large pillows, and "heel" with these pillows, walking straight ahead and pivoting into turns until they feel comfortable making snap-pop corrections. If you are using a metal training collar, the sound it makes when you make a proper correction will be similar to that of the action of a zipper. If on the other hand, you hear slow, separated clicks when you make a correction, one of two things is wrong. You are not making the corrections fast enough, or you are not using a proper metal training collar with flat links that have good action.

Needless to say, to administer corrections the right way you need to have a training collar that fits. There should be three or four inches of slack left when the collar is pulled snugly around the dog's neck. If you have an extension of more than three or four inches, your training collar is too large. Since it is too large, it will take that much longer for you to telegraph, through your leash and training collar, the corrections you want the dog to receive.

Some trainers feel that the sheer physicality of an initial heeling session is enough, and the trainer should keep mum. This approach emphasizes the responsibility of the dog to follow the handler no matter what. It seeks to play on the dazed dog's nerves. Having tried this method, we have found that many dogs simply crumble if heeling is done in silence. They need to focus their attention on the handler. Dogs need the human voice during initial heeling work more than at any other time and they need encouragement that is properly timed.

We suggest that you really open up and talk to your dog when you begin to heel. If your dog is coming along with you more or less peacefully, just whisper gentle encouragement, bending over slightly, making eye contact whenever you can. But if your dog forges ahead, or hits the end of the leash, pop the dog back into place sharply, and at the same time say, "Good, boy!" or "That's my girl," just as the dog feels the correction. Be sure to make this exclamation very loud and happy. The dog will be momentarily disturbed by the negative correction coming from your leash, so your positive verbal correction must be loud enough to balance

things off. What you are doing is providing negative and positive reinforcements at the same time, to achieve your objective of keeping your dog near your left leg. This will involve careful timing on your part. Under no circumstances should you verbally scold the dog for going out ahead or lagging. Use your voice *positively* in your heeling work. Keep the dog turned *on*, not off.

As you begin to make turns, encourage the dog a second or so before you turn with a suspense-filled voice: "Okay, Duke, we're going to turn now, ready? Okay, here we go." Then make your turn, snapping your dog near if the dog strays. Keep telling the dog to pay attention, using short phrases like "Watch me," or "Look here." Don't be afraid that a lot of verbiage will confuse the dog or hide the key training words. Separate the word "heel" from the rest of your vocal dissertation by a few seconds, but keep up that steady stream of praise and directives. If you are thinking of going into the obedience ring with your dog, you should realize that only the command words are allowed in the ring. As you progress in training, scale down your amount of talk, so you will be ready for the comparative silence of the ring. But if you are not planning to enter obedience trials, keep talking.

The response of some dogs to the heel will be to clutch their owner's left leg in fear. Others will begin to play "top-toe" by placing their paw on the handler's left foot, ready to move out when the handler does. If you get either of these reactions, especially the first fearful response,

When you stop on heel, ease the dog into a sit. Push down on the dog's rear and pull up on the training collar simultaneously.

take it a bit slower. Chances are, you've been too hard on the dog physically while failing to include enough verbal encouragement. Stop, praise the dog, take a break together. Remember, every dog is an individual, and no single method of teaching any exercise is absolutely right for every dog. Whenever you are training, stop every so often and "read" your dog. Is the dog comprehending what you are doing? What do the dog's eyes look like? Is the dog looking up at you? Never train any longer than twenty minutes. Two or three sessions a day are fine, separated by several hours.

Forging ahead will be the most common problem you face when training your dog to heel. You can try any number of corrections for this. As your dog begins to move out after some distraction, or just by sheer whim, grasp the leash tightly, hold your arms close to your body, and turn sharply to the right. At the same time give a loud encouraging vocal correction, "This way, that's my boy!" or something to that effect. For older dogs with chronic forging-ahead problems, it is often helpful to pass the leash behind you from the left and come to a complete stop. Proceed only when the dog is by your left side. Your left turns will no doubt be less precise than your right turns. If you have a dog that clutches your leg or hugs too close on left turns, give the leash a jerk away from your body as you turn. This will help move the dog out away from your body, preventing a trampling accident. As you continue to practice turns, have someone else watch you

work with your dog and point out areas that need improvement. An alternative is to train in front of a large plate-glass window or a sliding glass door and observe how you and your dog move as a team. Don't try to train completely alone. Constantly check and recheck your training guide, or consult an instructor. One woman who had her dog trained at New Skete returned one afternoon to show off her teamwork with her cocker spaniel. Following our instructions to conduct a twenty-minute training session daily, she had trained her dog to a near-perfect heel — with the dog walking on her *right* side. We reminded her that the dog had initially been trained (correctly) to heel to the left of the handler, and that this had been carefully explained in a demonstration and in literature accompanying our course. "Oh!" she exclaimed. "*That's* why I had so much trouble getting him to heel!"

As we said before, anything can happen when you begin to work on the heel. Let's cover some other possible problems in more detail. If your dog is walking on the wrong side initially, you might try steering the dog over to the left, stopping and praising the dog when in the correct position. If this trait continues and the dog seems to make a game out of it, a showdown is imperative. When your dog has sauntered off to the right, turn abruptly to the right and walk right into the dog. Your dog will yelp, the leash might get wrapped about your leg, and general panic might ensue, but your dog will realize what a fix it is in and return to your left. If the dog does begin to go back

Correct forging ahead by popping the training collar sharply and walking the other way.

Chronic forgers can be halted by passing the leash behind you and leaning back into it as you come to a dead stop.

to your left, help the dog out by untangling the lead quickly if it is fouled, or by spryly moving out of the way so the dog has a clear path of return. Once the dog realizes its mistake and tries to correct the situation, make sure you *let* the dog correct itself. An important rule in training is that there are definite moments when you must *let the dog win.*

Leash-biting is another common heeling problem. In this situation the dog responds to correctional snaps by attacking the leash. Probably it was never properly exposed to a leash as a puppy. Incidentally, if you wish to avoid a multitude of heeling problems, introduce the leash to your pup at a young age (see Chapter 27, on puppy training). If you purchase a pup over three months old, inquire whether it has been exposed to walking on a leash and what its response is. If your dog snaps at the leash, stop cold and discipline the dog under the chin. When you begin again, stoop down close to the dog, move your hand to the point where leash and training collar connect, and proceed slowly. The dog is then guided rather than pulled. Another solution to leash-grabbing is to decrease your physical corrections and increase your positive vocal reinforcement. Don't slacken off completely, but try to minimize your physical corrections and maximize your vocal encouragement, until the leash-biting stops.

"The Mule Act" is another common response, in which the dog braces its front and possibly hind feet and refuses to budge. The solution: keep going. Don't try to "talk it out" with the dog. Simply turn around,

make eye contact for a moment, and announce, "Let's get going." Give the "heel" command again, then *walk.* Remember, if you stop longer than a few seconds and try to have a heart-to-heart coaxing session now, you are ultimately doing yourself and your dog a disservice. Dogs who stage the Mule Act are often leader-type dogs who are used to taking their supposed "masters" for walks. Remember, in all obedience exercises, you are reordering your leadership relationship with your dog; so, at some point you are bound to be at odds.

The dog that decides to bite the handler when being leash trained cannot be tolerated and must be physically disciplined. The second the dog uses its mouth on any part of your body, no matter how gentle or seemingly unintended the nip, stop and discipline the dog under the chin, as described in Chapter 10. *Don't* wait. After you have completed your discipline routine, including physical contact, eye contact, and the Alpha-wolf roll-over, give the heel command again and continue on your way.

Remember, you must curb all of the above problems as they happen. Don't wait until the next sessions. Your first heeling session might go smoothly, or it might be chaotic. Prepare yourself before you begin by reading all, not just part, of this book, making sure you understand the instructions. Practice heeling with inanimate objects (pillows, innertubes, or even cooperative humans on all fours are good dog substitutes) to help you sharpen your technique before you work with a dog. Finally, approach your initial heeling session calmly. Meditate with deep-breathing exercises just before you begin. Try to "center" on your objective of walking as a team with your dog.

The automatic sit is part of the heeling process, and it can often be trained in conjunction with the heel. As you heel, you may notice that your dog sits near you when you stop. If he or she does, praise the dog warmly. You can encourage a more or less automatic response by remembering to pull up slightly on the training collar as you stop, gliding the dog into a sit. If your dog does not show this tendency to sit automatically, use the following tactic. As you come to a stop, transfer your leash completely to your right hand, pulling up on it. With your left hand, reach down and back and press down on the dog's rear

end, easing the dog into a sit. When the dog seems to be getting the idea, eliminate the left-hand push-down and use both hands to pop up the lead. When you begin to work on the automatic sit, resolve that your dog will sit each time you halt. Don't compromise, unless you really want the dog to remain standing. You will appreciate your work on the automatic sit when you come to a curb of a busy street and your dog sits without command, or when you are juggling a baby or a bag of groceries in your right arm and need to walk your dog with only your left hand on the leash. Dogs that heel correctly and sit automatically are a joy to introduce to guests. All that need be added is the "shake hands" trick for a truly impressive canine greeting!

31 The Sit and Stay

If your dog is accomplished at heeling and automatically sitting when you stop, you have already essentially mastered the sit. Training your dog to sit and stay should be swift. If your dog still has trouble obeying the command "Sit," then correct the dog using the methods discussed in Chapter 30, on heeling. If your dog is not sitting at this point, perhaps you have been too lenient in your corrective pop-ups with the training collar, or

not quick enough to press down on the dog's rear end. Speed up your work a notch, and begin adding the command word "sit" in a very emphatic tone.

There is one hand signal and one word common to all trainers in teaching the sit-stay. As they give the stay command, they bring their right hand in a sweeping motion directly in front of the dog's eyes, halting just before the dog's nose without touch-

The hand signal for stay. Have the leash taut as you give the command "Stay."

Then step out in front of the dog, keeping the leash taut.

Later, drop the lead and use both hands to signal the dog to stay.

ing it. Try this blocking hand motion on yourself a few times by bringing your hand toward your own face in a quick, sweeping motion. Stop sharply just before you reach your face. Your hand should be open, but your fingers should be closed together. You will note that the effect is dramatic — stay put. Make sure that your stay hand signal is quick. New handlers sometimes give the command several times, hesitantly, and then give a halfhearted hand signal with the palm of their hand barely open. The dog naturally breaks the stay.

With your dog sitting on your left, give this hand signal with your right hand, and with your left hand hold your leash straight up, applying a little upward pressure. (Bunch up the lead before you give the hand signal so that there is only about six inches of extension, plus the three or four inches the snug training collar will allow.) Keep your hand stopped short before the dog's face for now, and your leash taut but not choking the dog. Give the "Stay" command as you step out with your right foot first and turn to face the front of the dog. Hold the stay for a few seconds, then return to the dog's side and praise the dog. Lessen the amount of tension on the lead as you progress. Eventually you can stop using the lead and rely on the hand signal alone.

If your dog has trouble comprehending your command and signal, and especially if the dog breaks the stay as you begin to move away, use the following method. While holding only the end of the leash, give the dog the command "Stay" and then swing around to the dog's front. Quickly raise both hands before the dog's face, lean over, and give the command again. Then, back away from the dog a few steps. Hold the stay just a few seconds, and then return to the dog and give praise. Take it very slowly, increasing the time of the stay and the distance you back away with each lesson.

If the dog breaks a sit-stay, the correction is always the same. Go and get the dog. Don't call the dog to you. Take the dog forcefully back to the exact spot where the stay was set, and repeat the command and signal. If you are quick, you usually can stop your dog from breaking a sit or down-stay by yelling a very piercing "*No!*" just as the dog begins to move. Just make sure before you verbally correct the dog that the move is a real break, and not simply a readjustment of position for comfort.

In your initial sit-stays keep your leash in hand, holding it loosely. Later, when you are more confident of your dog's staying power, drop the lead, but leave it on. This will help you retrieve your dog in the event of a break. During a sit-stay, sustain eye contact with the dog to keep encouraging the dog to look at you. If the dog's attention wanders, whisper softly and dramatically, "Watch me, watch me," to refocus the dog's attention on you. Provide simple distractions at first. Sidestep lightly, or toss up a ball or rock. If you are working in a class, or with friends, try working in a circle, with the handlers bunched up in the middle and the dogs on sit-stays on the edge of the circle, facing in. For an effective distraction, the handlers can then rotate once and return to their original positions. Dogs who are weak on the sit-stay should be placed between dogs who are solid in their staying power. This will help the weak dog to learn to stay. For now, simply return to your dog after a sit-stay. Make sure when you return you circle around in back of the dog, ending so the dog is on your left side. Break the sit-stay with an animated "Okay," and give your dog praise if the exercise was performed correctly. When your sit-

Keep telling the dog to watch you, but don't be surprised if he isn't too thrilled at first!

Provide distractions to help your dog to learn the stay. Keep eye contact and focus the dog on you.

If you work on sit-stays in a group, do it in a circle with the handlers bunched in the center.

stays are solid, you can utilize them in training what is perhaps the most crucial of all obedience exercises, the recall.

32 The Recall

Most dog owners want two things from training. They want their dog to come when called and to lie down when asked. They may perceive other training exercises as ornamental and not connected with the dog's ability to come when called and to lie down and stay. But there can be no real recall unless there is a sit-stay to practice it from, and no real lying down unless there is a down-stay. It is on the recall that owners of leader-type dogs will experience difficulty. This type of dog will need extensive work.

Since dog training must be approached within the context of the overall dog-owner relationship, don't expect the techniques in this chapter to guarantee perfect performance in your dog unless you correct the other defective aspects of your relationship at the same time. For instance, don't expect the dog to run to you happily in a formal training session if you persist in calling the dog to you for punishment when it is off lead. If you have ever in the past called your dog to you and then punished it, resolve now to avoid this at all costs. *Never* call your dog to you and then dish out punishment. Always go and get the dog if you must reprimand it.

Begin to practice the come while you are heeling. As you heel, step back suddenly three or four paces and call the dog in to you. Your dog will be surprised at this interruption of the heeling pattern, and may continue to forge ahead. As the dog hits the end of the line, reel the dog back to you, saying "Come!" As the dog nears you, pull up on the training collar, as you did in training for the automatic sit, and have the dog sit in front of you. Now bend over and praise the dog.

When the dog is coming in well and sitting automatically in front of you, you can begin to give the command and the hand signal for stay; then walk around the dog and back to the position with the dog on your left side. Then repeat the routine several times. When you are sure the dog has the idea, put the dog on the sit-stay and move out from the animal. Do this slowly, holding the leash taut over the dog's head at first. Later, move out farther, and drop the leash. Hold the sit-stay for at least thirty seconds.

You are now ready to call the dog in. This is a very important moment. What you do now can influence your eventual off-lead control of your pet for better or for worse. The tendency now (and the actual instructions in many training manuals) is for the handler to stand erect like a wooden doll, and stiffly pronounce the command "Come." Depending on the instructor, the dog's name may or may not be included in the invitation.

How often have you seen a frustrated housewife standing on her porch, hands on hips, stern expression on her face, and in an even sterner tone of voice, repeatedly calling her wayward dog? Meanwhile, assuming the dog even hears the command, it may be bounding about playfully or perhaps crawling to its master fully expecting a trouncing. Many a dog owner pronounces at this point, "See, he *knows* he's done wrong — just look at the way he comes to me!" If these dog owners could see themselves calling their dogs, they would realize that no living, feeling being, canine or human, would want to come in to a person with that kind of bodily and vocal expression. Not surprisingly, we have found that some handlers who train like puritans and call their dogs like military sergeants often train and call their children in the same manner. If you are experiencing chronic difficulties in getting your dog to come to you, there might be something wrong with *how you look* when the dog sees you calling.

With your dog poised on a sit-stay, stoop down on one knee, eye level with the dog. Open your arms wide, creating a funnel effect, inviting the dog. As you open your arms, call the dog. Use both the dog's name and the word "come!" As the dog nears you, rise slightly but stay near the ground. Invite the dog into your arms and give it a warm welcome. Immediately after you say the word "come," plant a smile on your face and try to make eye contact with the dog. Keep smiling until the dog reaches you, and then explode in laughter and praise.

Vary the length of time you wait until you allow the dog to break the sit-stay and come in. Chances are, your crouched position will encourage the dog to waddle into a sit as it nears you. If your dog is so ecstatic

that it jumps up on you, allow this at first, in order not to dampen the dog's enthusiasm. Later, gently ease the dog down into a sit. The main point is getting your dog to respond to the word "come!" Every time it does, the dog wins a big victory. Problems like jumping up, urinating from excitement, or happy rolling around on the grass can all be solved later. You are headed toward the goal of having your dog come in happily and sit in front of you, as is required in the obedience ring and useful in home situations. But at first, it's acceptable to put up with any monkeyshines the dog may perform when coming in. Again, the moment the dog enters the confines of your arms is very important. Let the dog enjoy it.

As you progress in recall work, lengthen the distance of your recalls. Begin to use a long twenty- or thirty-foot rope, attached to the dog's training collar or leash. Put a weight on the end of this rope, so you can toss it out from you or to another person more easily. Sit the dog, give the command "Stay," and toss the rope out. Leave the dog's side after the toss. Call the dog in to you as described earlier. If your dog shows the slightest hesitation in coming in, pop the rope sharply. If necessary, reel the dog in. Don't worry about the dog getting tangled up in the rope it is dragging — he'll make it without too much difficulty. Praise the dog exuberantly when he reaches you.

When you are confident that your dog fully understands the word "come," begin to add distractions. Get an assistant to toss a number of

*Use your long line to practice distance recalls. Throw your weighted line out, then
give the command "Stay."*

objects in the dog's path, such as a bone, a ball, or another pet. Correct interest in these diversions with a sharp tug on the long rope. Don't be afraid to repeat the command "Come" more than once, and to use other orienting sounds like hand clapping, pounding the ground, or a set of keys. But if the dog's mind is wandering, don't waste any time popping the rope to bring him in.

Having your dog come and sit in front of you will depend both on how well you have made eye contact with the dog when it heard you call and on your reaction to the dog when it is in front of your crouched body. In the beginning, you can allow some playfulness, but begin to encourage the dog to sit in front of you while you stroke its head and shoulder regions. Give the sit command if necessary, but try to ease the dog into a sit by an upward tug on the training collar and by petting the head area. We do not want the dog to be dependent on the command "Sit" when it comes in. We want the dog to glide into a sit on its own initiative. When the dog is sitting in front of you consistently, continue to "funnel" the dog into you with your open arms, but as it nears you, rise to your full height slowly. When the dog nears you and sits, give the stay command and hold the pose for a moment. This is excellent preparation if you intend to teach your dog the "Finish" in which the dog returns to your left side by walking around your body, or by side-hopping back to the left. This exercise is included in books that specialize in obedience ring exercises. The average dog owner might consider the "Finish" ornamental, but it is a nifty exercise that can be very beautiful if performed correctly. We recommend Wynn Strickland Carson's method of teaching it. Her books are included in the reading list.

To transfer to the off-leash recall, secretly detach the rope leash after giving the stay command and tossing out the rope. If you do this correctly, the dog will think the leash is still on. Then proceed as usual. Some dogs sense immediately when the leash is off and decide to cancel the rest of the obedience session. If this is the case, you may have goldbricked on your initial recall training and need to do more on-leash work. Dogs who sense that the leash is off and decide to make a break for it should be retrieved and immediately taken back to the same training area. If your dog really takes off and there is no chance of getting it back on the training field, chalk up the experience, but when the prodigal returns, ignore the dog completely. After a half hour or so of the cold shoulder, give the command "Come" in a friendly tone. This is an effective way of teaching the dog without breaking our cardinal rule of never disciplining the dog when it comes to us.

If you can retrieve the wayward student and return to the training area, place the dog between two handlers and call it back and forth. The handlers should start with only five or six feet between themselves and the dog, extending this distance when the dog comes in correctly. Use the long rope if necessary, tossing it

Crouch down to call the dog. Have your arms wide open and smile. Praise the dog lavishly when it reaches you.

Later, rise to your full height as the dog comes in and sits in front of you. This is the correct position.

back and forth. With this method, the dog feels encased, and one or both handlers can stop any getaway attempts more conveniently than one handler working alone. The round-robin recall is also recommended for dogs with runaway tendencies.

33 The Down

We prefer either of two methods when teaching the down. Both involve easing the dog into the down position rather than forcing it down, and both involve body contact. Many people have great difficulty training the down, which is actually a simple exercise. It is often approached as a punitive exercise, with irate handlers attempting to ground their dogs by stepping on the leash or strangling the dog until it lies down. This frustrates both handler and dog.

Milo Pearsall's methods of training the down are humane and easy, and most importantly, they work. Our methods are a variation of the Pearsall method. We have found the small differences in our methods to be effective, especially in teaching large breeds to lie down. Begin by heeling a bit with your dog, and then come to a stop with the dog in a sit position. Make eye contact by stroking the right side of the dog's face, which will encourage the dog to look up at you. Mention calmly, "Okay, ready for something new?" Make your voice animated and happy. Many handlers become tense when they begin to teach the down, anticipating that they may have trouble and actually inviting it in the process. Immediately tell the dog to stay, and kneel down beside the dog. Hold the dog around the middle for a minute for reassurance. With your right hand grasp one leg just below the elbow, and place your left hand on the dog's upper back. Give the command "Down!" in a firm but animated voice, and move the leg forward, simultaneously pushing down firmly on the dog's upper back. Do not make the motion abrupt and coarse — make it smooth, easing the dog down. If you need to, practice this exercise with a human on all fours before attempting it with the dog.

Once the dog is down, kneel nearby, stroke the dog, and give a short speech of praise. Keep your tone of voice low but affectionate or the dog will try to get up. Keep one hand on the back region, applying light pressure. In the early stages, end the exercise after thirty seconds or a minute, praising the dog when it rises. Decide on some key word like

Teaching the down. Move one leg forward and simultaneously push down firmly on the dog's upper back.

"Okay!" to signal the dog to get up. When the dog seems to be steady on the down, you can begin to rise from the ground yourself, but keep one hand in contact with the dog's back. Correct attempts to get up by applying pressure on the dog's back and saying, "No, down!" If your dog moves quickly and manages to squirm up, go through the whole process again, then rise more slowly, applying pressure as you get up. If your dog tries to move backward as you lower its front, block this motion with your left leg or knee placed squarely behind the dog's rear end. Don't be afraid to use all parts of your body in training. Your legs can become auxiliary arms if you know how to use them.

Some larger breeds (German shepherd dogs, Great Danes, St. Bernards) might need even more body contact and pressure to insure a smooth down. For these breeds, or for dogs who fight the first method, try a slightly modified approach as follows: lift *both* front legs together, with your hands just below the dog's elbows, and lower the dog's front. At the same time, lean over and into the dog, putting your left knee on the dog's back. The first few times, you may find this movement uncoordinated, but with repetition it will become smoother. Since your face will be quite close to the dog's, you can reassure the dog easily and even use your chin to help lower the dog's head. The motion is the equivalent of falling on top of the dog, without actually doing so. Once you have the dog down with this method, proceed as above. With some particularly

rough types, who refuse to stay down for any length of time, you may simply stay on your hands and knees, straddled over the dog, until you are confident that the dog will stay.

If you are able to stand up for three minutes and the dog stays down, consider the exercise partially learned, and begin to teach the release, which is to sit. To end the exercise, say "Okay!" and slap the upper part of your thigh, encouraging the dog to rise. Stationed on the dog's right, you will be able to block any attempt to come to a full stand by having your left hand aimed toward the dog's rear end, ready to push it down.

When you complete a down, no matter what its length, be sure to praise the dog lavishly. Stroke especially the side of the face closest to your body, which will encourage the dog to look up at you. Make eye contact and sustain your verbal praise for a while.

There are two potential problems that may develop when training the down. Your dog may come to depend on your manipulating him into position, and come to think that the point of the exercise is to wait to be lowered. For this type of dog, stop lowering the animal and apply pressure on the training collar while giving the voice command. Keep one foot over the leash when the dog is down to prevent it from rising.

Occasionally there is the dog who shows absolutely no comprehension of the down command and will remain sitting with a "What, me?" expression on its face. One way to find out if the dog has an idea of the exercise or is bluffing is to place a dog

Another method of teaching the down is to lift both front legs and lean over and down on the dog, easing it into the down.

treat in front of his feet and give the command "Down." If the dog will go down for food, he can go down without food. Let him have the treat this one time, and resolve to be firmer in teaching the down in the future. If the dog does not go down for the food, it is most likely confused and afraid to make any moves. Backtrack and train the down from the beginning.

34 The Down-Stay

If your dog really knows the down, then the down-stay should follow naturally. Most dogs do not like to lie down and get up immediately. When they settle down, they mean to stay for some time. The practice of circling two or more times before "landing" is common to many breeds, especially German Shepherd dogs. The dog appears to be carefully selecting and surveying the eventual resting place. If you are training for the obedience ring, you will have to eliminate this practice by teaching an immediate down and insisting on an unwavering down-stay. A sloppy down or fidgeting on the down-stay will cost points in the obedience ring. If you are not training for the ring, you may decide to permit quirks like circling before lying down, lolling about or rolling over on a down-stay, or extensive yawning ten seconds into a down-stay. The dog is not bored. a position that encourages rest. begin work on the down-stay,

give the command "Stay," and the hand signal, as in your work for the sit-stay. Then circle the dog while keeping one hand in contact with the dog's back. Circle twice and release your hand, but do not allow the dog to get up. Repeat this circling process, applying pressure with only the tip of your index finger. You will be stooping over as you circle the dog. The dog may try to look behind at you as you circle. Allow this, but don't allow any attempts to rise. Curb these immediately by placing your whole palm on the dog's back and pressing down immediately upon any sign of rising, saying "No, down, *stay*." When you feel confident, go around the dog without stooping down or applying hand pressure. Don't be afraid to repeat the command "Stay" several times if the dog shows any interest in rising.

Remember, there is nothing wrong with the dog looking around at you as you circle and go momentarily out of

Stay in sight while your dog does the down-stay. Avoid eye contact now — or the dog will think you are inviting it to come.

Nothing surpasses working in a class for steady down-stays. Here the monks and nuns toss a ball down the line of handlers while the dogs hold the down-stay.

An agile handler can sprint over the dogs while they hold down-stays. Distractions are necessary in all areas of training.

sight. But don't encourage this trait by talking to the dog from the rear. Once they understand what is going on and what is expected of them, most dogs will simply look ahead and wait while the handler walks around. When your dog gives you this type of reaction and no longer appears worried or jittery about staying in one place, you can begin adding distractions to make sure the down-stay is steady. Begin by stepping over the dog, back and forth, several times. Throw a ball or twig in front of the dog, repeating the command "Stay" as you throw the object. If you can work in a class, an agile handler can leap over each dog in line. In a class, the dogs learn from each other not to move. Most of our puppies at New Skete learn to lie down and stay at a young age without any formal training simply by watching their mothers and older dogs on down-stays when the monks are dining. A dog who is just learning the down-stay sometimes does better if sandwiched between two experienced dogs who are steady on the exercise and distraction-proof. These self-assured dogs will help allay the fears of the novice dog and help it to hold the down-stay longer.

The correction for breaking the down-stay is always the same. Go and get the dog. March it back to the same spot and place it on the down again. Hopefully, you will be able to stop the dog in its tracks by a hefty "No!" which may pin the dog back to the ground before it moves more than a step or two. If the dog lies back down on its own initiative, it is not necessary to replace it in the same spot.

Next to the recall, the down-stay is probably the most useful of all the exercises in formal obedience training. Begin to integrate this command into the dog's daily routine. Have the dog lie down and stay while you eat dinner, read, watch television, or during any sustained activity. When company visits, allow the dog to greet your friends, and then place it on a down-stay nearby. Don't expect immediately to isolate the dog from you and expect it to hold a down-stay. This takes a lot of practice. If you plan to go on to CDX (Companion Dog Excellent) level in the obedience ring, your dog will need to be able to hold a down-stay with a group of dogs for five minutes while you are out of sight. If you are building up to this level of training, you are most probably also working with the high jump. If you occasionally hide behind the high jump while your dog is on a down-stay, the dog will never be sure whether you are behind it at an actual obedience trial.

In a household situation, the down-stay can be used for dogs who bother company or display aggressive reactions to humans or other dogs. Practice training your dog to the point where the down-stay is perfect. Dogs who know and can sustain the down and down-stay rarely need to be shunted off for any reason. They can be told to lie down and stay, and are able to be peacefully included in the family circle. This is a distinct pleasure for both dog and owner.

About Obedience Competition

If you and your dog become totally proficient in obedience work, you may consider entering the obedience ring. The American Kennel Club offers a Companion Dog (CD) title, Companion Dog Excellent (CDX), Utility Dog (UD), and a Tracking title (T). There is now an obedience championship title also (OTC). A booklet describing the obedience regulations can be obtained from The American Kennel Club, 51 Madison Avenue, New York, New York 10010. Since these regulations sometimes change, request the most recent edition. If you are seriously interested in obedience competition, you should subscribe to one or both of the periodicals specializing in obedience work, listed at the end of this book. You should also join an obedience club. Try to find a club that specializes in obedience training, and if that isn't possible, join the training branch of a local breed club. Obedience training, on the whole, provides an opportunity for mutual growth, on the human as well as canine level. As the proud breeders and trainers of many titled obedience dogs, we think you will enjoy the world of professional obedience competition as much as we have. There is one catch: you and your dog must be *good* to get anywhere in professional competition.

If you are considering obedience competition, make sure that you and your dog are able to work as a *team*. Don't enter the ring until you know the exercises and are completely ready. If you jump in too quickly, you will probably fail the trial, waste the judges' and other entrants' time, and possibly do damage to your dog. Take your dog to fun matches before you go to a real obedience trial.

Puppies intended for obedience work should be purchased from reliable, behavior-oriented breeders who breed for brains. These youngsters should be exposed to early KPT training and taken to fun matches early in life. Remember, though, it is seldom too late to attempt to win the CD title or a higher title. If you feel you are "ring-ready" and still do not qualify with the necessary one hundred and seventy score, don't be discouraged — chances are, you mishandled your dog. Check with the judge when he or she has a free moment. Most judges will tell you what you did wrong, and many may give you helpful advice. Above all, don't become bitter or disappointed. These reactions have a way of affecting training. Your dog will pick up these reactions immediately and they will damage your overall performance. Remember too that you are competing for points and not against other handlers and their dogs. If you want to compete in the obedience ring, you must have a sense of humor. You must be able to laugh at yourself and your dog. The first thing you will learn, sometimes painfully, is that your dog has some faults, and that your dog is not the center of the universe and the idol of all. These two realizations alone are worth all the time and effort that goes into obedience competition.

While this book is not specifically intended for obedience competitors as such, we feel it can be useful to them in enabling them to "read" their dogs more effectively, and to help them perfect the exercises involved in winning obedience titles.

The American Kennel Club puts it succinctly in their introduction to the obedience regulations: "The purpose of obedience trials is to demonstrate the usefulness of the pure-bred dog as a *companion of man* [italics ours], not merely the dog's ability to follow specified routines in the obedience ring." If you decide to enter obedience trials, keep your mind on that purpose and goal.

Problems

36 House-training

There is no area of dog training where more myths abound than house-training. House-training should be a simple procedure, but for many owners it is a drudgery that sometimes never ends. It's surprising the number of clients we see who have owned dogs for over two years and confess, "He's really never been house-broken." Later, we come to find that this can mean that the dog has the problem on a daily, and even twice-daily, basis. If house-training had been approached correctly and consistently at first, the problem would have been short-lived.

MYTH NUMBER ONE: When you find a mistake, rub the dog's nose in it. DO NOT do this, ever. You will defeat your own purpose, risk infecting the dog, and encourage stool consumption.

MYTH NUMBER TWO: When you find a mess you should hit the dog and then ostracize it for a good long period. Nonsense.

MYTH NUMBER THREE: After you find a mess, take the dog to the place where elimination is supposed to occur, stand over it, and scold it. This is all backwards; the dog needs praise and encouragement at this location, not punishment.

MYTH NUMBER FOUR: You can train a dog to eliminate on papers or outside, or both. This myth causes more confusion than any other. Dogs need a *consistent* approach to house-training. We never suggest paper training unless the situation is truly extreme and the dog has *no* access to the outdoors. (For instance, you live ten floors up and there's no elevator, or you reside in a fallout shelter.) We find paper training is usually a short-cut for the owner, a convenience at the time, that later backfires if it is even successfully comprehended by the dog to begin with. If at all possible, train your dog to eliminate in one spot, outdoors.

Here is our approach to house-training and house-soiling incidents.

1. The basic rule is to capitalize on your dog's natural desire to keep its nest clean. This is an inherited characteristic. Anticipate when the puppy or dog wants to go out. The signs are: nose grazing, obvious squatting, loitering around the door, constant activity. The times are: every two hours for pre-twelve-week puppies (except when they are asleep), after waking from a nap, fifteen minutes to one half hour after eating, before riding in a car, after drinking a large amount of water.

2. In general, we suggest regular feedings for pups and older dogs, depending on veterinary advice. We find the "nibbler plan" (food down all day for the dog to eat at will) often encourages house-soiling. For pups we suggest water be offered at regular intervals, *not* left down all the time. Water and food should be taken up at night, giving the pup enough time to eliminate before it retires. Do

not leave water down for a dog until you are sure of absolute sphincter control.

3. Respect your dog's biological clock. Be consistent in the times you let it outdoors. Remember: to a degree, many activities will have to be coordinated with the dog's biological schedule until it is mature. Sleeping in, late parties, vacations, shopping trips, and other activities may have to be based on when the dog will need to go out.

4. If you discover a mess, go and get the dog. Do not call the dog to you if you discover an accident, but go and get him. We do not feel that you must catch the dog in the act, and if you don't, clean up the mess. The dog needs to have its attention focused on the mess before you clean it up. Try to take the dog to the mess as soon as possible. If you observe the dog getting ready to eliminate don't shriek or freak out — swiftly sweep the dog up and outdoors, even if this means an elevator trip. Most dogs will stop short and hold it until they get outside.

5. If it's too late for that, bring the dog to the mess by the collar. Sit the dog near the mess. Make the dog look at it. Direct his eyes toward it. Keep the dog sitting.

6. If you are just beginning house-training, do not make a big thing over the punishment but scold, growl, and make the dog feel the effects of your displeasure. For older dogs with chronic problems, physical discipline may be in order.

7. Take the dog forcefully to the proper place and deposit the dog

there. This is essential since the dog must connect on where to eliminate. Stay with the dog, if it's not possible to leave it alone.

8. After you return, clean up the accident with paper towels or other absorbent materials. Paper plates cut in half make good emergency cleaning aids. Wash the area with a twenty-five percent solution of white vinegar and hot water. Odor neutralizers, like *Nilodor* and *Lysol,* can be used after the vinegar treatment. It is important to remove the scent from both human and canine detection. Block off the area if possible until it is dry. An overturned chair will do. *Do not* let the dog see you clean up its accident. This encourages the "maid syndrome" in bossy pets, which is at the root of many serious house-soiling problems. You are not the maid, in residence to clean up after the dog. Nor are you the doorman, there to let the dog out whenever it demands. While house-training means anticipating your dog's desires, it also means the dog must learn sphincter *control.* You will defeat this development if you play maid or doorman. After a mistake, don't isolate the dog or keep scolding it. Avoid any overfondling of the pet at this time, unless in response to a command (come, sit, stay, lie down). If you are experiencing difficulties in house-training a puppy or older dog, seek advice from a qualified trainer who will sit down with you and map out an approach for your dog. Avoid harsh physicality in disciplining house-soiling, and rely instead on preventative measures.

37 Chewing, Digging, and Jumping Up

CHEWING

If breeders did a better job of preventing early chewing, their puppies would have fewer problems when they go to new homes. As with many canine troubles, the problem starts at an early age. Some breeders do not provide chew toys but instead allow their puppies to chew on portions of the whelping box or kennel. All it takes to stop this kind of behavior is a loud "No!" and replacement of the object being chewed with an acceptable one. Providing hanging and toss toys helps puppies through their teething stages. However, when the puppy goes to a new home, the breeder should advise the owner to focus the pup on one toy only. Troubles connected with puppy chewing are further explained in Chapter 27, on puppy training.

Several commercial products are available to help puppies and older dogs stop chewing. They work on the premise that some dogs withdraw from unpleasant smells such as citronella or tabasco. A new repellent containing methyl nonyl ketone is effective. Grannick's Bitter Apple Lotion is an old standby of experienced trainers and breeders. But don't count on sprays, ointments, or magic salves to relieve you of chewing problems. While they may help to a degree, the best method of chewing control is early vigilance, a sharp reprimand, and disciplinary action.

The length of time destructive behavior has been going on will determine how quickly and easily it can be corrected. Chewing correction in older dogs is sometimes more difficult. Destructive chewing usually takes place when the owner is away. One of the staple descriptions we hear in our discussions with training clients is the scene they meet upon returning home from work. We have heard horror stories of drapes pulled down, pillows torn open and the contents liberally strewn about, mattresses with their centers hollowed out, plate-glass windows smashed, and wall-to-wall carpeting ripped up. Once the canine mouth gets going, there is no limit to the destruction it can do. Perhaps the most amazing story we have heard concerned a two-year-old Newfoundland–St. Bernard mix that knocked over the refrigerator, ate five squares of linoleum tile, and ripped the phone out of the wall. When the owners returned, the dog had the audacity to growl at them. Your particular tale of woe probably pales next to this one, so cheer up — something can be done!

We have found a common pattern in owners' reactions after these discoveries. First, they are surprised, even if the dog has done damage before. Next, they are angry and inaugurate a wild chase scene with the dog, sometimes ending with physical punishment, more often in the dog's escape. Even more commonly, they scold the dog as it cowers in a corner and the owners resign themselves to cleaning up the mess. Many owners explain the behavior by saying, "He hates me for leaving him alone," or a variation on that theme. They are partially right.

The fact is, however, that usually the dog does not "have it in" for the owner. It may experience frustration on other levels. The factors that produce chewing sometimes originate in the environment and not in the dog. Once these factors are understood, it is easier to solve the problem. The dog's chewing can then be focused on an appropriate object, and the destructive behavior stops.

First, the owner must regulate emotional homecomings or departures. Greet and say good-bye to your dog quietly, affectionately, but not overdramatically. The owner should instill a sense of responsibility in the dog by training it with the words "Watch things," or "Watch the house," when leaving, and giving gentle praise when arriving home. A program should be set up so that the owner leaves for only five or ten minutes the first day, twenty the next, and so on. Each time the dog manages to stay alone for even a short length of time, it is a big victory and a stepping-stone to longer stays. Leaving the radio on for a short time sometimes helps to distract the chewer and make it think the owner is going to return soon. Owners of chewers should immediately stop pleading with their dog not to chew. The dog's

supply of treats should be cut off immediately. Don't attempt to bribe the dog into good behavior. Start obedience training the dog, at least to the come, sit, and stay level.

Physical discipline for chewing is not always effective, although some swear by it. They suggest taking the dog to the scene of the crime, focusing its attention on the chewed object, either by picking up the chewed article or bringing the dog's eyes down or up to it, and disciplining the dog under the chin lightly. This method has some merits, we feel, but only if it is coupled with preventative measures such as chew-proofing the house, using repellents, and correcting the faulty aspects of the dog–owner relationship. It is a good idea to attempt to make the object being chewed unpleasant in itself, and avoid, if possible, connecting up discipline with the owner. One way to do this is by use of repellents and another is to set mousetraps strategically in the chewing area. Don't worry, they won't get stuck on the dog's nose. They can accomplish two objectives: when you are gone, they can act as reminders to the dog to stay away from a given area, and when you return home you can gauge your progress simply by looking to see if the traps went off.

Remember to approach the problem positively too. Provide the dog with a nylon or rawhide bone. Make this bone a special toy. Play fetch with it. Wiggle it on the ground in an inviting way and let the dog chase it. Keep this bone away from the dog for at least two hours prior to leaving home. Just as you leave, rub the bone between your palms for two minutes. This will put your scent on it, you will remember. Then offer it to the dog as you leave. Make sure the dog sees you offering it. If the dog takes it from you, so much the better. Do not provide the dog with chew items such as leather shoes, socks, or personal items.

Avoid disciplining chewing by other techniques, such as taping the chewed object in the dog's mouth (a good way to get bit), hitting the dog with the chewed object (the dog won't get the connection), or tying the chewed object around the dog's neck (the dog might chew on it again), all methods which have been used from time to time.

To correct chewing, first reorder the relationship between you and your dog by establishing yourself as the Alpha-figure. Obedience-train your dog. Suspend all treats. Provide effective discipline if you discover a chewing incident. Focus the dog on an acceptable chew toy. All other techniques, such as sprays, mousetraps, screamed or shrieked "Noes," and prayers are simply adjuncts to the above basic approach.

DIGGING

In a dog that is orally oriented and socially isolated but kept indoors, chewing is the usual result. In almost all of the digging dogs we have worked with, the underlying cause of the digging was also social isolation. Dogs who are forced out into the backyard, often "for their own good" or "to get fresh air," soon resort to frustration-release activities, and dig-

ging is one of the most popular. Since digging is often related to social isolation, the most positive step the owner may take is to allow the animal into the house. Obedience training, diet regulation, and other changes are to no avail unless the dog is included in the owner's life.

Interviews with owners of diggers often reveal that the dog lives in the backyard "because he drives everyone crazy when he's indoors." Sometimes the owners cannot even remember when the dog was last allowed inside. In other cases, the dog is allowed inside only at night (when the owner is ready for retiring) and excluded from all other activities. Obedience training, preferably including the down and down-stay, is imperative if the dog is allowed into the house on a steady basis. If you are experiencing a digging problem, begin a program of obedience training immediately. Some methods intended to solve digging are filling the holes with water and shoving the dog's face into them, installing chicken wire in the holes, rigging the holes electrically, and other popular corrections. Invariably, we have not had much success with these corrections unless the owners stop banishing the dog from the social circle.

Digging can, occasionally, be related to breed type. Some Siberian huskies and other sled-dog breeds seem to enjoy digging cooling holes. Dachshunds and other breeds genetically geared to go underground may show a predilection for digging. Pregnant bitches will often begin burrowing activities as they near their whelping date. Most dogs respond well to a program of simple obedience com-

In the jumping-up correction, grasp the dog's front paws and quickly bring your knee up into the midsection. Do not use this correction on puppies.

mands, and by being included, rather than excluded, from social activities inside the house.

JUMPING UP

Why do dogs jump up on humans? Usually they want attention, and have learned that they get it when they meet their owners face to face. There are many prescribed solutions to this common problem. The most popular is the knee-in-the-chest routine. The trouble with this correction is two-fold. First, it should not be the first correction administered, and second, when it is done, it is usually executed so poorly that the point of the correction is completely lost on the dog.

It's far better to start correcting this problem in puppyhood by teaching the sit. Establish a rule for the entire family-pack that no jumping is allowed, whether you are wearing dungarees or a white suit. When you sense the pup is ready to jump up, tell it to sit, and put your palms out flat in front of its face to block jumping. When the pup sits, praise it.

Older dogs may need a more physical approach, but begin by simply grasping their paws when the dog is up on you and squeezing them tightly. Then let go and tell the dog "No!" The dog will soon get the idea that jumping up leads to an unpleasant episode. Remember, one good correction will save you fifty ineffective ones. If you tell the dog not to jump, follow through the first time it jumps up, not the second or third.

A word of caution about the popular knee-in-the-chest correction. It should be reserved for chronic cases, not for puppies or occasional jumpers. To execute it correctly, begin by observing the knee kicks of drum majors at football half-time events. When the dog jumps up on you, immediately grasp its paws and hold them. Bring your knee up into the dog's mid-region and make firm contact. Simultaneously push your arms out and heave the dog out and away from you, saying "No!" as you do. It is not so much the physical force involved that is important as it is the element of surprise and drama. Again — caution — this is not for puppies or sporadic jumpers. Try the other preventative methods first for those types. Domineering owners may seize upon this correction in order to teach the dog not to jump "once and for all." This may backfire and have detrimental effects on your overall relationship. Don't try to teach your dog to stop jumping up without teaching it the sit at the same time.

38 Protection Training and Attack Training

If you are considering having your dog attack-trained, you may want to ask yourself the following questions. First, why do you want this kind of training? What do you know about this kind of training? How many other dogs have you seen with this kind of training? Is there a difference among "attack" training, "protection" training, and "Schutzhund" training — or are they all the same? Will you be able to control your dog if you have it attack-trained? Are you covered by insurance for any harm your attack-trained dog might do? Finally, ask yourself: does your *dog* need this kind of defensive training, or do you?

There are several methods of attack training. Most, but not all, consist of a system of heaping "last straws" on the dog. These systems demand that the dog be put under stress and agitated until the dog decides, "This is it! I'm not going to take it anymore!" resulting in growling, barking, or eventually, a full charge attack. This basic agitation is then channeled into verbal and hand signals — key words and gestures — such as "Get him," "*Fahss*" (in German), and a raised arm, on which is usually worn a protective sleeve. Rarely, if ever, are the stereotyped words "kill" or "attack" used. The dogs are also taught "out" — to back off completely. The above is a simplification of attack training, and to many trainers, it is a sophisticated art.

You are obviously placing your dog under a considerable amount of stress if you opt for this kind of training. Consider whether your dog can sustain stress. If it cannot, attack training could have very negative side effects. Remember to evaluate your dog privately before asking the attack-dog trainer for an opinion on your dog's potential abilities. Some trainers will "attack-train" almost *any* dog, given enough time, the right method, and a paying owner. Others will be very honest with you, and will tell you if your dog cannot take this kind of training, or whether they feel you could not handle a dog with this kind of training.

Many owners want their dogs attack-trained because they feel threatened. Life in a big city and in other crime-infested areas can be frightening, and men and women living alone need protection. But whether formal attack training is in order depends on the owner's concept of a dog's responsibilities. Should a dog feel responsible *for* a person or *to* a person? There's a big difference. Some trainers who specialize in attack training will tell you in candid moments that a good dog will defend its owner naturally, without specialized training. Often the mere presence of a dog discourages intruders.

Protection training often backfires. Take the dog who is conditioned to bark at the slightest sound. When burglars "case" a house or apartment and the dog barks consistently at every sound, they need only make a few discreet inquiries to see what the real story is. One woman had her Doberman trained to bark at any sound around her home. She came to us in desperation after three robberies. The neighbors were complaining since they could no longer stand the constant barking. One neighbor unsuspectingly informed robbers about the dog's barking. The burglars posed as future neighbors and asked about the dog. "Oh, *him*," the neighbor replied, "he barks all the time, at anything, she had him trained that way at some school. But all you have to do to shut him up is yell at him, assuming he can hear you. I hope the house you're moving into isn't around here — we have to wear earplugs!" The gentlemen did move in — right into the Doberman's house the next day, while the owner was at work. A stern "Shut up, mutt" quieted the dog, who resumed barking after the robbers left. The neighbors made nothing of it.

"Learned aggression" is often a problem with protection-trained dogs (see Chapter 40, on aggression). Occasionally we'll receive for "de-programming" an attack-trained dog that has gone overboard and misinterprets his verbal and hand signals. This kind of retraining is often difficult, and unless the dog has discrimination, poise, deductive reasoning, and stamina in its genetic background, it is difficult or impossible to instill it.

An attack-trained dog is like a loaded gun. It should be handled only by experienced persons in appropriate situations. We commend the use of German shepherd dogs and other breeds in police units across the country. When used *defensively* they can be of great value. These dogs belong to qualified handlers, are trained to high standards, and are sound genetically. Laymen, on the other hand, should not have attack-trained dogs. They are not qualified to handle the animals.

Obviously, we do not recommend protection or attack training. Schutzhund training, developed in Europe, might hold out a possibility for viable defense training. It is a three-fold obedience system, encompassing tracking, obedience, and protection skills. In true Schutzhund training, no one area is overplayed or allowed to overbalance the others. This training system treats the dog as a whole. It proceeds from the correct premise that the dog is responsible to the owner. Schutzhund handlers make the protection phase of training more of a game than anything else, even though it can be of use in real-life situations. While there are some eccentrics within any movement, and currently much division within this particular one, Schutzhund training is a sound training method and *may* be of value to your dog.

However, you must begin with a sound, healthy, discriminating animal, usually from one of the working breeds. You must delve deeply into the training method to become a qualified handler. This will mean joining a Schutzhund club.* It is not pos-

* For information on the Schutzhund movement in the United States contact United Schutzhund Clubs of America, 3924 Sylvan Ave., Modesto, Calif. 95355, and NASA, North American Working Dog Association, 1677-7 North Alisar Avenue, Monterey Park, Calif. 91754.

sible to explain Schutzhund training in full here, but it is a good possibility for those who feel they need protection training.

You will notice that many ads for attack-trained dogs play on the owner's basic insecurities, promising "freedom from worry" and "complete safety." Methods of training that do not relate to the whole dog and fail to educate the owner do a disservice to dogs and society. If you are interested in protection training, please think twice.

39 Alarm Barking

In the preceding chapter we come down hard on the standard types of attack training. But this does not mean that we are against pets announcing the presence of visitors and, if necessary, protecting their owners from physical harm. We are breeders of German shepherd dogs, and work hard to preserve the structural and temperamental integrity of that breed. We prefer that our dogs have the instinctual drive to bark and defend. That's usually enough to ward off intruders.

Owners who want protection from their pets must learn to use their pets psychologically to best advantage. The major factor in many a tight squeeze, such as a robbery or assault attempt, is the victim's ability to bluff the attacker. Bluffing with your dog means portraying the dog as a true friend and defender, and not as the weak, timid critter it may actually be. If you are being followed or bothered, it's a good ploy to bend over dramatically and whisper something to the dog. For a direct approach, hold the dog tightly by the training collar and say, "Not yet, not yet," to bluff intruders. Remember, the average intruder has no way of reading a dog correctly and cannot tell that it is bluffing.

If you want your dog to bark on command, begin teaching it when it is a puppy. Hold a treat over the dog's head, and when it sits, tell it to "speak!" Encourage the dog to vocalize, and if it gives you even a whine or whimper, treat it promptly. Some young puppies fall naturally into the game, and older dogs sometimes take more time to train.

When you are confronted with an unpleasant situation, assuming your dog is not already barking because of it, you can fake holding a treat and get a few barks that way. The other person usually cannot decipher what is a friendly or unfriendly bark, and most likely will not want to take the chance to find out.

To train your dog to bark aggressively at an intruder, set up situations where someone unknown to the dog can help you. Have your accomplice cover his or her face with a nylon and wear a heavy coat and strange hat. The hat is the main thing that will trigger the barking reflex in many dogs — make sure it is a bizarre hat. Have this decoy make some motion outside the house that sets the dog off — rattling a door knob, jimmying a lock. You should be sitting quietly yourself, reading, with the dog nearby, preferably lying near you. When you hear the sound, alert and look at your dog. If your dog gives a slight grump, consider the exercise over for that day. If the dog does not react, you may go over to the door with the dog, encouraging it to inves-

tigate. As the dog sees the stranger, it may growl or bark. Have the stranger reel backwards, linger for a moment, and then run away, as if they were "running away" from the ferocious dog. Then kneel and praise the dog for "saving" you from the intruder. Repeat this procedure on a weekly basis, but don't let things go too far. Remember, all you want is a warning growl or bark. If you already have problems with these two activities or if your dog has a problem with aggressive behavior, don't condition it any more with these set-ups. Remember too, that many breeds have a built-in propensity for protective behavior and it is a matter of waiting for this trait to mature. Don't expect a three-month-old puppy to be Rin-Tin-Tin.

40 Aggressive Behavior, or How to Deal with a Canine Terrorist

Canine aggression is one of the most frequent problems we deal with when dog owners bring their dogs to us. After seeing hundreds of aggressive dogs, we have come to view them in much the same way we see political terrorists or hijackers. Their aggressive reactions are often seemingly

unprovoked, unpredictable, and unexplainable. Like some political terrorists, some dogs seem to use aggressive behavior for display only. If really confronted, they back off. Others, however, if cornered, will explode.

Let's not underestimate the scope

of canine aggression. It is a serious problem. In urban centers, dogs that roam freely resist anyone who attempts to round them up; they roam about, picking up new "recruits" along the way, teaching them aggressive techniques. In the country, packs of dogs loot chicken houses, attack sheep, run livestock, and challenge farmers who attempt to catch them. And every suburban neighborhood probably has at least one or more well-known "weird dogs" whose aggressive behavior is fabled by the residents of the neighborhood. Ask the question "Have you ever been bitten by a dog?" of practically anyone, and the answer, if yes, will also include typical details of the incident. Very frequently the situation involved a strange dog that was unsupervised at the time, along with some action by the bitten party that the dog interpreted as threatening.

Training techniques cannot solve every case of aggression. But good training techniques and counseling can diagnose and evaluate aggressive behavior and attempt counterconditioning. We cannot stress enough: if you are having a problem with aggressive behavior, see a dog trainer as soon as possible. Preferably, see a trainer on a one-to-one basis, so that the trainer can work individually with your dog. Do not attempt to "cure" aggressive behavior simply by enrolling in a park obedience course. Go to a trainer or counselor who can evaluate your dog's behavior individually. Get help as soon as possible. Don't wait, thinking the behavior will go away or get better. It rarely does without

training. The behavior usually gets worse.

It is important that the trainer know all the details of any aggressive incidents. It is essential that you evaluate the incidents, preferably with a trainer. It is possible to work alone, but it is more difficult. Get a notebook and write as objective and unemotional a description as possible of what happened in each incident. Describe the people involved, the time of day, the actual split-second sequence of events (as best you can recall), and what discipline (if any) you administered. Note down where the incident took place and the extent of the damages. It is important to know if the dog broke the victim's skin, or nipped, scratched, or inflicted the damage with its mouth or paws. Many times we've had clients report mouth bites only to discover later, when taking a case history, that the injury came from the dog's toenails or paws, and not from the mouth at all. Check and recheck. Don't justify or condemn the dog's actions. Simply record the facts. This is the first step in determining the seriousness of the problem.

After figuring out the sequence of events in the incidents themselves, it is now possible to attempt to categorize the aggressive behavior. There are several types of aggression.* Listing them may help you to determine what kind of behavior your dog exhibits. Remember, your dog may be

* Dr. Benjamin Hart, "Types of Aggressive Behavior," *Canine Practice* (May-June 1974), p. 6.

expressing more than one of these types of aggression at the same time.

FEAR OR SHYNESS AGGRESSION

By far the most common type, fear aggression occurs equally in males and females and is usually seen in situations of stress and noise, where the animal would escape (leave the area) if at all possible. Instead it is forced into a confrontation with another dog or a human. For instance, owners who drag a reluctant Fido up to "meet" strangers, instead of conditioning the dog more slowly to accept company, invite an incident of fear aggression. Most incidents happen in stress situations when "display" reactions mushroom into actual incidents. Obedience training, at least to the come, sit, and stay level, is necessary, since the lack of leadership is often instrumental in aggressive behavior. We have our greatest success in treating this type of aggression by diet changes (basically to a high-protein, low-carbohydrate diet) and obedience training. The round-robin recall is often very helpful. Some veterinarians have experimented with drug therapy for this kind of aggression and have had varying degrees of success. Librium and Valium are sometimes used. Ovaban, a drug used to control estrus, is also used. Do not attempt to administer drugs to your dog without veterinary assistance. Drug therapy can sometimes simply mask underlying problems in the dog–owner relationship which are the root cause of the behavior.

TERRITORIAL AGGRESSION

The second most popular form of aggression is the front-yard and back-yard variety. To a degree, in-house and in-car aggression is natural. Owners often put the dog in a bind, encouraging territorial aggression and discouraging it when they find it excessive. The dog may be confused. Remember, alarm barking does not mean the dog should bark at everyone. You must draw the line for your dog with a sign-off phrase like "No more!" or "Okay, that's enough." The best procedure is to inhibit territorial aggression in pups with a stern "No" and friendly exposure to strangers. This type of response usually crops up in the pups around the fourth or fifth month. Be on the lookout for the reaction and clip it immediately. Postmen, meter readers, and other "intruders" might be instructed to stoop down and play fetch with the puppy or dog, neutralizing its uptight response by acting happy around the dog. The owner should not encourage territorial barking by the puppy or older dog. Greet visitors in a happy way. Obedience-train the dog for control. Warn the aggressive dog in a stern voice *before* admitting strangers to the house. If the incidents get out of hand, discipline as described in Chapter 10, including the Alpha-wolf roll-over. Any excess growling, barking, or suspicious whining should be disciplined verbally. Biting, charging, chasing, and pant-leg nipping should be disciplined both verbally and physically.

INTERMALE AGGRESSION

Males generally fight other males. The problem is an inescapable canine situation related to testosterone secretion and the environment in which the males are raised. This complaint is frequent among dog owners whose dogs meet up with free-roaming neighborhood males. To control this, defecation and urination by a male must be restricted to the dog's immediate area. This is so that he does not mark off the whole neighborhood as his private domain, which will easily lead to confrontations with other males who intersect his kingdom. Castration has been reported to reduce this behavioral trait.*

AGGRESSIVE RESPONSE TO TEASING

This is a situation when children, and occasionally adults, taunt a dog until it retaliates. It is sometimes common when neighborhood gangs team up to pick on a particular dog, often when the owners are away. Children should be cautioned not to scream around dogs. They should never chase a dog, even one they know. Children should never pet a strange dog. Adults who tease dogs or accept "dares" to approach a dog ask for what they get. One young man accepted a dare to stick his hand into a car occupied by a Doberman he did not know. He was bitten and wanted to know why!

* William E. Campbell, *Behavior Problems in Dogs*, p. 107.

PAIN AGGRESSION

Pain aggression often occurs at a vet's office when the dog is given a shot, wheels around, and bites the vet or vet assistant. Elevating it to an examination table is often enough to set some dogs off into a bite reaction when injected. Though veterinarians may insist on examination-table treatment, many such isolated bites and aggressive displays can be solved by on-the-floor exams. If you have a problem with this type of aggression, ask your vet in advance to treat your dog on the floor if elevation to the exam table is not essential. Only a veterinarian with a slipped disc should refuse. Another type of aggression, which we have frequently seen, is the result of pain induced by hip dysplasia, auto accidents, or other injuries. For animals with these in their background, aggression when getting up to a standing position, especially if forced, is a possibility. We have seen many cases where large breeds have been involved in biting incidents when a child sits on the dog's hind quarters when playing, causing the dysplastic or previously injured dog to wheel around in pain and bite. The only way to check for dysplasia or injury is to go to a vet and have your animal x-rayed. Treatment can often be as simple as aspirin administered twice daily, or as complicated as an operation to relieve the tension.

LEARNED OR "TRAINED" AGGRESSION

Chapter 38 in this book deals with the pitfalls of protection and attack training, not the least of which is the danger that the dog might misuse his acquired aggressive skills. Owners considering attack or protection training certainly should think twice about it. "De-programming," while possible, is difficult. Rehabilitation of these canine soldiers usually entails a separation from the owner, an emphasis on animated, happy training sessions, and avoidance of the cue words and hand signals the dog might have been conditioned to respond to with aggressive behavior.

GENETIC AGGRESSION

As professional breeders, we have an insight into the possibilities of genetic aggression that some trainers do not have. This is an extremely difficult area to diagnose. For instance, genetic aggression often looks like fear or shyness aggression. A good trainer will take into account the possibility that the aggressive behavior has genetic roots. He will take the time to check the dog's bloodlines, if he can secure the pedigree from the owner. Almost every breed has what breeders call "freak bloodlines" that produce dogs with a propensity for aggressive reactions. Chances are, one or both parents had trouble in this area. The owner can usually recall something about the behavior of the sire and dam. Experience can sensitize a trainer to detect genetically based aggression, but it is still very important for you to provide the trainer with all possible information about the dog's ancestors if you suspect this possibility.

Maternal aggression, which crops up when a bitch has a litter and over-defends it from all comers, seems to be passed from mother to daughter. If this was a problem with the mother of your female and you plan to breed the daughter, reconsider your plans.

Again, we stress that if you are interested in a puppy, buy only from a reputable breeder. Try to meet the sire and dam of your puppy personally — not from behind a kennel cage, but in normal house circumstances if at all possible. Many dogs bark and *look* aggressive when "behind bars." If the breeder is hesitant to take the dog out of the kennel, or if the sire or dam shows aggressive response, reconsider buying a puppy from their litter. Don't think that an aggressive father will instill courage in your puppy. You may get much more than you bargained for. Purchase a sound puppy from sound parents and a conscientious breeder. Obtain a guarantee on temperament. This is the only sure way to side-step the chance of genetic aggression.

41 Behavior in and out of Cars

RIDING IN CARS

We often hear about the dog that "can't ride in a car." Dogs that vomit, whirl around, bark incessantly, or attempt to jump out of a moving vehicle are becoming a more frequent training problem. As urban and suburban auto use rises, we find more dogs who are unable to adjust to the stress of riding in a car. Usually these dogs were not properly conditioned to riding as young pups. The poorly trained puppy develops a fear of cars at worst, and at best, a lifeless resignation to riding.

The First Ride To avoid these reactions in a new pup, ask the breeder whether the pup has been exposed to riding in a car. Tell the breeder you prefer that the pup's first ride not be the ride home with you. Some breeders use foresight and load up a whole litter early after weaning to take them out for a short spin. Make sure the puppy has not eaten for at least three hours prior to leaving with you. If you have children, explain to them that the puppy will need quiet on the way home. During the pup's ride home with you, avoid any unnecessary coddling. Place the pup on the floor or on the seat next to you on top of a thick pile of spread-out newspapers. Do not respond to whining by petting (rewarding) the puppy. You cannot punish the puppy for any

vomiting that may occur now – it is an involuntary reaction. If you scold and punish the pup, you will make it even more nervous about riding in cars. We often suggest that our clients simply drive to the bottom of our hill, stop under a shade tree, and rest a moment with the pup before continuing home. If you are going over twenty miles, stop for five minutes to give the pup's stomach a rest. The point is to try to get the pup home *before* it gets sick.

Teaching the Dog to Ride For your initial trips, choose a smooth, straight road. Withhold food and water for at least three hours beforehand. Prior to starting out, let the pup sit in the parked car for five minutes. Proceed in the manner described above with short trips, ending in a play session. Gradually lengthen your trips until your dog can go over twenty miles without any sign of heavy salivating or indication of vomiting.

Whether puppy or older dog, your attitude about riding in the car affects your dog. Owners who coddle their dogs, overuse tranquilizers, or sympathize with stress-whiners actually encourage car problems. You should praise the dog excitedly as you near the car. As the dog jumps in (or as you load it in), give the dog a good deal of physical and verbal praise. After that, your job is to drive and the dog's job is to ride.

Dogs that are too active in the car need to be taught to down and stay before any lengthy rides can be attempted. If you have a puppy, teach the pup according to the methods outlined earlier. If you have an older dog that is a problem in the car, teach the down according to the methods described in the obedience section. Superactive types should have a leash on at all times when the car is moving. They should not be allowed in the front seat, and a partner should be taken along on initial trips to enforce the down-stay. Do not tolerate any barking from young puppies. Clench the pup's mouth shut, and if the barking escalates, stop the car completely and discipline the pup.

Older Dogs with Car Problems If you have an older dog with an established barking problem, try this method. Begin on a normal trip with the dog on leash, and deliberately drive past situations that you know will trigger a barking reaction from your dog. Just as the dog begins to bark, say "NO!" loudly and stop the car. Plan in advance to slam on the brakes (obviously after making sure no driver is behind you). If your dog slides forward as you stop, falling into the front seat, you have the right idea. But you're not done yet. Grab the leash and open the car door. Take the dog outside and discipline it physically and verbally, under the chin, as outlined in Chapter 10, or if you prefer, add the "shakedown." The whole pattern of shouting "NO!", stopping the car as quickly and dramatically as you can, and disciplining the dog must follow quickly and smoothly.

When you reload the dog, place it in the Alpha-wolf position as described in Chapter 10. Make eye contact with the dog while it is pinned in this position, and tell it, in no uncertain terms, that you intend to stop and discipline it whenever it barks. By the time you are done, your dog should be quite dazed. Now drive on about a block and turn around and drive right past the same distraction as before. "Read" your dog's reaction in the rear-view mirror. If the dog appears anxious to bark, slow down, and warn the dog. At the first sign of any whining or barking, stop the car and repeat the routine.

You may wonder if the above procedure would be more effective if you drove and had a partner execute the corrections. It might be, but we have seen many cases where a recalcitrant car barker clams up when the driver is accompanied, only to burst out in a flurry of barking when taken on a "solo flight" with one person who is busy driving.

Popular corrections for car hysteria include rattling a can full of pennies or stones, blowing a whistle, or using an ultra-sound device. Besides the fact that your control over the dog then depends on the presence of an object, these methods, in our experience, are usually stop-gap measures. Then, too, a dog in the middle of a freakish fit, barking wildly and lunging at a car window, cannot easily hear *anything*, including the owner's screamed or shrieked reprimands. Since overbarking inside cars often has to do with poor puppy conditioning and with a faulty dog–owner relationship, the discipline should stem *from the owner* to be effective. Remember, as discussed in the section on discipline, use your hand to discipline the dog, not an object.

CAR CHASING, BARKING AT CARS

Dogs that chase cars usually suffer from hyperactivity or from sheer boredom. Sometimes, these dogs are protecting their own territory. This behavior is reinforced each time they chase a car and it "runs away." Depending on the length of time the problem has been going on and the intensity of the dog's chases, correction may take several weeks. The best policy is to clip this behavior quickly when you first notice it in your puppy. Often puppies will simply bark at cars or other moving objects, such as bicycles. The pup perceives the moving object as threatening. Pups should be exposed to moving vehicles, on leash, at a young age. Walk along a busy street with the pup at your side. Stop and encourage the pup if it looks hesitant about cars. Never allow the pup to be called by persons in a car or on a bicycle.

Chronic car, bicycle, horse, or other-dog chasers need a correctional regime that spans several areas. Popular corrections like heaving a water balloon at the dog from a car window, throwing BB's in its face, or using a squirt gun to ward off car attacks may be effective with some dogs, but these can too often be simply stop-gap measures. The correction should come from the owner in a two-fold approach. First, a renewed relationship with the dog emphasizing obedience exercises and the leadership of the dog owner. The dog must be trained to the sit, stay, and come level, *at least*. Preferably, the dog also should learn to heel and lie down on command. Second, a staged confrontation between dog and owner when the dog is chasing a car.

To concoct this confrontation, leave your critter attached to a leash for two days. Just let the dog walk around with the leash on. Begin by having daily obedience sessions, emphasizing sit, stay, and come. Leave the leash on after the session. You will need it later. Secure the help of a neighbor with decent driving skills, especially the ability to brake quickly and dramatically, but safely. Make sure this helper has a car that is strange to the dog. If you examine your dog's behavior, chances are there are certain kinds of cars that trigger the chase reflex more than others. We once knew a sheepdog that was partial to pick-up trucks and Cadillac sedans. Try to arrange to have a "hot car" for your confrontation. Talk over your dog's behavior with your helper before this training exercise. Map out the dog's behavior on a sheet of paper, noting the position of the car and dog when the chasing normally begins. Some dogs are erratic. They may begin to chase a car when it rounds the bend a block from the house, but others will act excited only when a car is directly in front of the house. Still others behave like clockwork, charging when each car is lined up in a familiar position. Whatever your dog's habits, prepare your helper for them, so that he or she will know when to brake.

When you are ready for your confrontation, physically and psychologically, select a second helper familiar to the dog to stay in the house. Prop open the door the dog usually uses just enough to assure the dog easy access into the house. Arrange to meet your first helper off your own property. Get in the car with your helper and when you near your own house, crouch down low in the backseat of the car. Place one hand on the door handle and be ready to fly out of the car as soon as your helper brakes and gives you the word. Your cohort should give you the word, "Okay, go!" as soon as the dog is in full flurry at the side of the car. At this point, the driver brakes the car hard, then you fly out of the rear door and make for the dog — *quickly*. If you are fast enough, the dog should be caught totally off guard. If not, you still have a chance to snare the dog by stepping on the leash as the dog exits the scene. The important thing is to get the dog. Why? Because you are going to discipline the dog. If by chance the dog does manage to get away from you and make it back to the house, have your second assistant stationed inside the house capture the dog and bring it out to you to the site of the car chasing. This should not be necessary — try your hardest to get the dog as soon as you get out of the car. Many of our clients have a practice "dry-run" minus the dog, to get the feel of opening the car door quickly and making for the canine culprit. A dry run also gives the driver a chance to practice braking smoothly, quickly, and safely.

Discipline should be administered in the manner described in Chapter 10. Keep the dog near the car. When you have completed the Alpha-wolf rollover, take the dog back to where it belongs, and put it on a down-stay there. If the dog doesn't know the down-stay yet, down it forcefully and step on the leash. Then signal your driver friend to go ahead. The driver should turn around and drive past the house again, with the dog watching. This procedure rarely needs repeating twice if it is approached with gusto the first time. Make up your mind: do you prefer hundreds of ineffective corrections, screamed and shouted "No, no's," or do you prefer to mastermind one dramatic, effective correction?

Bear in mind that car-, bicycle-, or people-chasing is often the result of two canine frustrations. First, the bored dog that is ostracized from the house for any considerable length of time will eventually vent its frustration in some way — chewing, digging, or chasing being the most common. Second, the dog strung up on a chain or kept behind a fence that has a full view of traffic can often develop barrier frustration aimed at free-moving objects. Of course, a combination of boredom and barrier frustration is twice as mind-boggling for the dog. Part of the solution to chasing lies in somehow eliminating these conditions. The simplest solution is to bring the dog into the house, where it belongs. If no one is home during the day, explore the possibility of enclosing a yard and installing a dog door. Some dogs may not need access to the outside at all and can be kept inside except for supervised exercise and defecation periods. The biggest hold-up preventing these simple solutions is the owner who believes the myth that dogs "need to be outdoors," or that "dogs need exercise all day and should be allowed to run free." Believers of these myths might as well resign themselves to the possibility of a lifetime of coping with chronic chasing activities.

42 Social Implications of Training

The Humane Society of the United States estimates that there are eighty to one hundred million dogs and cats in the country. Two to three thousand more are born every hour of every day. Last year alone the nation's shelters had to euthanize thirteen and one half million dogs and cats. The pet population in this country is obviously out of control.

It is the responsibility of all dog owners to control the reproductive potential of their dog, whether it is a male or female. Spaying or neutering your dog is imperative unless you have serious breeding plans. If you do, please consider them carefully. Litters are hard work — take it from us; we've whelped and raised about one hundred of them. The puppies demand time and patience. They must be socialized, trained, and placed in proper homes. It is serious business. By no means breed your dog because you feel it would be good for it, or because you want your children to see the miracle of birth.

When you train your dog, you are helping to stem the pet population explosion. Dogs that are obedience trained have a healthy rapport with their owners. These dogs generally come when called, which is one way of preventing unwanted backyard breedings. Properly trained dogs serve an important public function, since they help to balance off, in the public's eye, the large number of badly behaved dogs. Obedience training encourages *good* breeding. Poor genetic specimens usually do not train well, but dogs that are bred for brains *and* beauty do. They act as advertisements for responsible breeders and divert business from puppy mills and pet shops. Obedience training can help us control the pet population explosion in this country which is reaching astronomical proportions.

When a Dog Dies: Facing the Death of a Dog

43

In the voluminous literature on canine health and training, very little has been written about the death of a dog and how the dog owner reacts. Yet the death of a beloved pet is a reality dog owners may have to face more than once. Part of training involves training yourself to accept the inevitability of your pet's death.

In dog owner consultations we have had an opportunity to discuss with many clients the death or imminent death of their pets, whether by natural causes, accidents, or euthanasia. It is never an easy experience for client or counselor. We feel that these people need someone to talk to about this, and should feel that the person to whom they are talking cares about their dog and the fact that the dog is dead, dying, or needs to be euthanized. Although the last thing they need is a cold clinical approach, sentimentality should not be wheeled in either.

While most veterinarians and animal workers are dedicated to protecting animal life, it is a well-known phenomenon that some professionals who work constantly in the face of death (human or animal) can develop an unconscious callousness and insensitivity to death itself and possibly to those closest to the dead and dying. To care demands a lasting sensitivity that comes with experience and reflection.

Most pet deaths are quick and painless and the pet owner does not really have time to absorb what has happened. Shocked by this quickness, they are sometimes guilt-ridden, angry, depressed. They may be suspicious of the veterinary profession, or they may blame the breeder for producing a poor dog, or the trainer for failing to modify behavior that eventually leads to death. For instance, the dog of one former training client ran out in front of a car after taking a training course. The client told the trainer, "If you would have taught my dog to come when called, it wouldn't have been hit by that car. You killed him."

Other owners swear never to have a pet again. Since we live in a society that teaches its members to become emotionally involved with their pets to an inordinate degree, reactions of disbelief, anger, and depression are common. In reality, we know that we usually outlive our pets — unless we are very old ourselves. Those are the facts of life. Dogs simply do not live as long as humans.

Perhaps the saddest deaths are the deaths of puppies, and next, the death of old companion animals that have lived with a master for many years.

All of us perceive puppies as fragile, mischievous, innocent, and delightful, yet we often fail to take proper care to protect a pup. Owners sometimes blame themselves for the poor supervision, improper nutrition, or other causes they perceive as the reason for their pup's death. If death results from internal causes or shortly after purchasing the pup, they may blame the breeder for selling a "defective" puppy — even if the breeder had no way of controlling or even knowing about the condition in advance. While it is fortunately possible to start with a new puppy, the biggest tragedy is the short-circuiting of the young life and the unresolved question of the pet's potential. The owner will always wonder, "What kind of dog would my pup have been?"

When a puppy or older dog dies, it might be assumed that the owner can handle the death with equanimity. This is not always so. If euthanasia is involved, the decision can be very difficult. It might be a course of action the owner never expected to have to take. He or she might have expected the pet's natural demise. Even if the animal does die of natural causes, the emptiness and gap in a household can be devastating. The monks at New Skete started their breeding program with the purchase of a bitch, after their original shepherd, "Kyr," got lost. The house was too empty without a dog.

GETTING ANOTHER DOG

The immediate reaction of many owners is to run out and get another pet. We have had people arrive at our breeding kennels in tears, on the rebound from the pound or veterinarian's office. They explain that they just lost their dog and want one "just like him." We have found that it is usually wiser for these owners to wait before getting another pet. The sad owner projects onto the new dog all of the qualities and talents of the deceased pet, forgetting that *each animal is an individual*. Occasionally a new dog will develop behavior problems and does not work out in the new situation. The owner may have unrealistic expectations of the dog, may constantly compare it to the former pet, and the resulting owner–dog relationship is off to a bad start.

While it is good to plan to get another dog at some point, we've found it is better to wait a month before actually bringing one into the household. In the interim, memories of the old pet start to fade and longing for a new one increases. Children, especially, will begin to agitate for a new pet. The owners may have an opportunity to talk about the old pet with a veterinarian or some other sympathetic parties. The veterinarian may be able to explain fully the medical causes of the pet's death, and give advice on what to avoid with a new one. Meanwhile, the scent of the old animal fades, which makes it easier on the new dog, since it could wonder why it smells, but does not see, the other dog.

THE DECISION TO EUTHANIZE

The decision to euthanize must be the owner's, but almost always there are others working on an advisory level who may be involved with the death. These people — veterinarians, trainers, specialists, animal-shelter personnel, and friends — must be especially sensitive to what the owner faces before and after euthanization. One cardinal rule is the owner must make the decision, not the advisers. The adviser's role is one of honesty — to explain alternatives.

If euthanization is indicated as one of these alternatives, it is the veterinarian's or specialist's role to expedite matters as quickly and humanely as possible. While simple good-byes are needed and wanted by some, not all owners want to say good-bye to their pet. This is especially true if the dog is being euthanized for behavioral reasons, and expecially if aggression is a factor. Advisers should not force an emotional "good-bye scene." Those acting in an advisory or helping capacity should make the death as painless as possible. If the injection method is used, it is good to explain this tactfully to the owners, and emphasize the lack of pain or suffering, and the idea that the pet simply falls asleep. This helps the owner to know the truth, and to handle subsequent emotions.

Euthanasia, obviously, is not easy for anyone, including the veterinarian or animal worker who has to perform it. Some veterinarians will not euthanize pets simply because the owners request it, especially if the owner says the dog has behavior problems but the owner has not sought out training. They may refer the owner to a competent trainer. Remember, veterinarians are dedicated to preserving animal life, not destroying it. So, if you have not worked with a particular veterinarian before, and your first contact is to request that your dog be put to sleep, you may get a flat no.

We encourage pet owners to be realistic about euthanasia. While it can be a difficult decision, it is usually not the end of the world. The hesitation to euthanize a pet that is suffering or has serious behavior problems, while difficult, pales when contemplated in the face of the mass extermination of millions of potentially sound companion animals. In our country, millions of unwanted cats and dogs must be eliminated, since there are not enough homes for all of them. These throngs of unwanted animals, with no possibilities of homes or owners, represent an abominable waste of life. They are a shocking indication of our lack of reverence for life.

The idea of pet burial is an individual question. For those interested there are pet cemeteries. We ourselves feel that pet cemeteries are a somewhat exaggerated expression of the emotions involved and a further waste of precious resources. We do not recommend them. (If your pet dies at home, most veterinary hospitals maintain crematoria where the remains can be decently disposed of.) For most people, photographs in a scrap book or a framed portrait serve the same purpose. There are many who prefer to keep the memory of their pet alive in their own minds, privately and discreetly.

A Parting Word

44 Dogs and New Awareness

I am secretly afraid of animals — of all animals except dogs, and even of some dogs. I think it is because of the us-ness in their eyes, with the underlying not-us-ness which belies it, and is so tragic a reminder of the lost age when we human beings branched off and left them: left them to eternal inarticulateness and slavery. "Why?" their eyes seem to ask us.

— EDITH WHARTON

Throughout this book we have stressed that a dog is a social being genetically geared to respond in submissive as well as dominant ways to human beings and other dogs. We have emphasized that as the owner, you should conceive of yourself as the dog's guide and Alpha-figure, including the dog in your activities as much as possible. If you can grasp the importance of these ideas, you should be able to enjoy a healthy relationship with your pet.

However, there is something more to be gained from your relationship with your dog. Your dog can provide you with a unique access to the natural world, helping you to expand your capacity for aesthetic appreciation, warmth, and enjoyment. We are dangerously out of touch with our natural roots. For many people, the only touchstones with the natural world still readily available are dogs and house plants.

On another level, relating to your dog can be a spiritual experience. We have avoided religion and religious jargon in this book, and we generally avoid mixing religion with dog training. Nevertheless, many of the ideas we hold about dogs have a deep spiritual basis. What lies at the basis of our love for dogs may be of particular interest to you, since it may help you to deepen your relationship with your dog, and with yourself.

An illustration of our "spirituality of dogs" is one of the great animal lovers of all time, Francis of Assisi, who has been an inspiration for all men, but more especially for those who wish to intensify their communion with nature. Saint Francis's love for animals is often romanticized to the point of sentimentality. The popular image of Francis sitting in the woods with sparrows perched on his shoulders, and rabbits, deer, and perhaps a wolf nestled at his feet is certainly a romantic exaggeration of Francis's amazing abilities with animals.

In reality, perhaps the *Poverello* himself did not fully understand his skill with animals, but he was very aware of his kinship with them. He did not leave us any "technique" to help us relate to animals more easily, but he obviously had the knack of communicating friendliness to animals through his body language. There is a way of approaching an animal so that the creature perceives the intruder as

Francis tames the wolf of Gubbio. Francis knew the secret of sensitive body language. Francis unified the world of animals and man in himself.

a friend rather than a threat. Francis tamed the wild wolf of Gubbio in much the same way that Daniel communicated with the lions in the den — by sensitive body language. This skill cannot be conveyed in books. In a sense, it cannot even be learned. One either has it or doesn't. Still, it is this skill that made men like Francis and the biblical Daniel so outstanding. By their inner attitude they unified the world of animals and man. Francis saw all creatures as his brothers and sisters, and for this, if for no other reason, he is a model for all dog owners, for the ecologist, the natural-

ist, and for everyone who wishes to develop this kinship with all life.

While Francis was a Western Christian, his responsive personality and affinity with all creation is in perfect harmony with the theology of the Christian East, which does not arbitrarily divide the world of animal and man, but strives to see the unity of all creation. The feast of the Transfiguration clearly portrays this idea. Christ climbed to the top of Mount Tabor with three friends, Peter, James, and John. There, he was transfigured in bright light before them, and the whole mountain be-

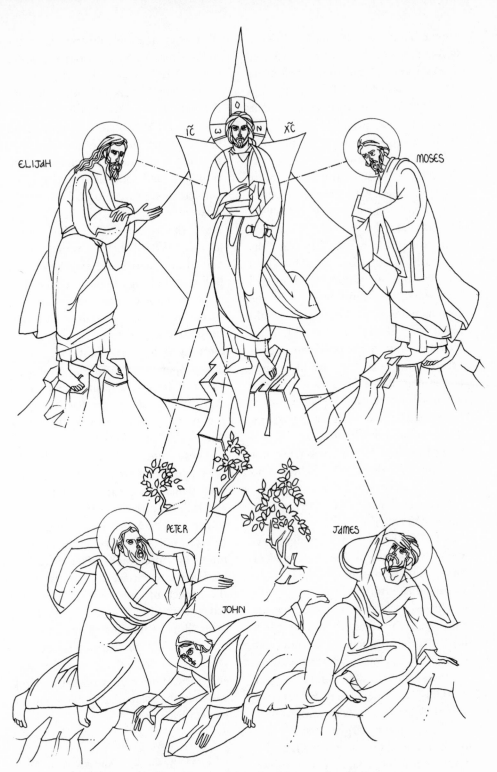

At the Transfiguration, all creation rises to a new level of awareness.

came radiant with that light. Christian thinkers in the East have interpreted this as a kind of call to all creation to rise to a new level of awareness. At the same time, Christ called each of us to change our behavior radically to meet this reality in our individual lives and circumstances.

Another Christian thinker of more modern times who stressed respect and compassion for animals is Teilhard de Chardin, the French Jesuit and paleontologist. Chardin felt that "the mystical vibration is inseparable from the scientific vibration," and looked forward to the transfiguration of the cosmos when men and animals would reach the "Omega point." While his writings are not specifically concerned with dogs, they are of interest to the dog owner because they stress devotion and respect for all creation.

As long as we insist on separating the world of animals and man, we will never be able to love animals truly, not even our own dogs. Where there is no love, no real stewardship and responsibility can develop, and these are essential. As Dr. Michael Fox says in his foreword, "Love is not enough." As soon as a person unifies the world of animals and man *in himself* he is ready to participate fully in life.

This is a theme that appears again and again in monastic history. We have mentioned one saint, Francis, but there are many more who were aware of their affinity with animals. Saint Anthony and the Desert Fathers are said to have tamed lions and wolves. In Russia, Saint Sergius, Saint Seraphim and others were on very friendly terms with the bears of the forest. The monastic fathers interpreted this phenomenon as an illustration of the monk's task to help restore the order that existed in paradise, the natural order, where man and beast, and indeed all creation, lived in harmony.

The idea that men and animals can live together in peace is an age-old theme. New ideas in conservation, ecology, and animal training that emphasize stewardship and sensitivity may have appeared just in time. As Kenneth Clark pointed out in a recent article, "What is needed is not simply animal sanctuaries and extensive zoos, but a total change in our attitude. We must recognize that the faculty of speech which has given us power over those fellow creatures we once recognized as brothers must carry with it a proper measure of responsibility. We can never recapture the Golden Age, but we can regain that feeling of the unity of all creation. This is a faith we all may share."*

These modest essays in training presuppose that we love our dogs, but they demand a great deal of thought and reflection from us. If our relationship with our dog is to blossom to its fullness, our sensitivity and awareness must be intensified. The invisible, ineffable current we call life must be the object of our love. As we ourselves share in it, so do other creatures. But we humans alone can work out the delicate harmonies in the score. If we do, we will indeed renew and enrich our own world, if in fact we cannot regain that golden age of perfect harmony.

* Kenneth Clark, "Animals and Men, Love, Admiration, and Outright War," *Smithsonian* (September 1977), p. 57.

If our relationship with our dog is to blossom to its fullness, our sensitivity and awareness must be intensified.

Selected Reading List

GENERAL BOOKS

Bergman, Goran. *Why Does Your Dog Do That?* New York: Howell, 1971.

Boone, J. Allen. *Kinship With All Life.* New York: Harper and Row, 1954.

Burton, Maurice. *The Sixth Sense of Animals.* New York: Ballantine Books, 1974.

Caras, Roger. *The Roger Caras Pet Book.* New York: Holt, Rinehart and Winston, 1976.

Fox, Michael W. *Between Animal and Man.* New York: Coward, McCann and Geoghegan, 1976.

———. *Understanding Your Dog.* New York: Coward, McCann and Geoghegan, 1972.

Holmes, John. *Family Dog.* New York: Arco Publishing Co., 1958.

———. *Farmer's Dog.* London: Popular Dogs Publishing, 1960.

Leach, Maria. *God Had a Dog.* New Brunswick: Rutgers University Press, 1961.

Lorenz, Konrad. *King Solomon's Ring.* New York: Thomas Crowell, 1952.

———. *Man Meets Dog.* Baltimore: Penguin Books, 1971.

McGinnis, Terri. *The Well-Dog Book.* New York: Random House, 1974.

Phaffenberger, Clarence. *The New Knowledge of Dog Behavior.* New York: Howell, 1963.

Schweitzer, Albert. *The Teaching of Reverence for Life.* New York: Holt, Rinehart and Winston, 1965.

Siegal, Mordecai. *The Good Dog Book.* New York: Macmillan, 1977.

Smythe, R. H. *The Private Life of the Dog.* New York: Arco Publishing Co., 1965.

Teilhard de Chardin, Pierre. *Man's Place in Nature.* New York: Harper and Row, 1966.

Trumler, Ebehard. *Your Dog and You.* New York: Seabury Press, 1973.

BOOKS ABOUT WOLVES AND OTHER WILD CANIDS

Fox, Michael W. *The Behavior of Wolves, Dogs, and Related Canids.* New York: Harper and Row, 1970.

———. *The Wild Canids, Their Systematics, Behavioral Ecology and Evolution.* New York: Van Nostrand Reinhold, 1975.

Mech, David. *The Wolf: The Ecology and Behavior of an Endangered Species*. Garden City: Doubleday, 1970.

———. *The Wolves of Isle Royal*. U.S. Government Printing Office, Fauna Series, number seven.

Mowat, Farley. *Never Cry Wolf*. Boston: Little, Brown, 1962.

Young, Stanley Paul. *The Last of the Loners*. New York: Macmillan, 1970.

———. *The Wolves of North America*. New York: Dover, 1964.

YOUR DOG'S ROOTS, BOOKS TO HELP YOU TRAIN SPECIFIC BREEDS

Beazley, John M. *Training Setters and Pointers for Field Trials*. New York: Arco Publishing Co., 1973.

Davis, L. Wilson. *Go Find! Training Your Dog to Track*. New York: Howell, 1974.

Holmes, John. *Farmer's Dog*. London: Popular Dogs Publishing, 1960.

Humphrey, Elliot. *Working Dogs*. The Dehack Effort, Box 922, Campbell, California, 1934.

Johnson, Glen. *Tracking Dogs, Theory and Method*. Westmoreland, N.Y.: Arner Publications, 1975.

Levorsen, Bella. *Mush! A Beginner's Manual of Sled Dog Training*. Westmoreland, N.Y.: Arner Publications, 1976.

Long, Paul. *About Training Pointing Dogs*. Slingerlands, N.Y.: Capital Bird Dog Enterprises, 1974.

Syrotuck, William G. *Scent and the Scenting Dog*. Westmoreland, N.Y.: Arner Publications, 1972.

OBEDIENCE TRAINING

Judy, Will. *Training the Dog*. Chicago: Judy Publishing Co., 1958.

Koehler, William R. *The Koehler Method of Dog Training*. New York: Howell, 1962.

Loeb, Paul. *Paul Loeb's Complete Book of Dog Training*. Englewood Cliffs: Prentice-Hall, 1974.

Martin, Robert J. *Toward the Ph.D. for Dogs*. New York: Harcourt Brace Jovanovich, 1975.

Miller, Dare. *Dog Master System*. Santa Monica: Canine Behavior Institute, 1975.

Most, Konrad. *Training Dogs, a Manual*. London: Popular Dogs Publishing, 1954.

Pearsall, Milo. *The Pearsall Guide to Successful Dog Training*. New York: Howell, 1973.

Saunders, Blanche. *The Blanche Saunders Obedience Training Courses, Combined Edition*. New York: Howell, 1976.

Scott, Tom. *Obedience and Security Training for Dogs*. New York: Arco Publishing Co., 1967.

Strickland, Winifred Gibson. *Expert Obedience Training for Dogs*. New York: Macmillan, 1965.

———. *Obedience Class Instruction for Dogs*. New York: Macmillan, 1971.

Tossuti, Hans. *Companion Dog Training*. New York: Howell, 1942.

BEHAVIOR PROBLEMS

Campbell, William E. *Behavior Problems in Dogs*. Santa Barbara: American Veterinary Publications, 1975.

Fox, Michael W. *Understanding Your Dog*. New York: Coward, McCann and Geoghegan, 1972.

Miller, Dare. *Dog Master System*. Santa Monica: Canine Behavior Institute, 1975.

Tanzer, Herbert. *Your Pet Isn't Sick. (He Just Wants You to Think So)*. New York: E. P. Dutton, 1977.

CHILDREN AND TRAINING

Benjamin, Carol Lea. *Dog Training for Kids*. New York: Howell, 1976.

Foster, Joanna. *Dogs Working for People*. New York: National Geographic Society, 1972.

Margolis, Matthew. *Some Swell Pup*. New York: Farrar, Straus and Giroux, 1976.

Peters, Heinz. *Bringing Up a Puppy the Natural Way*. New York: Vantage Press.

Pinkwater, Jill, and Manus, D. *Superpuppy, How to Choose, Raise and Train the Best Possible Dog For You*. New York: Seabury, 1977.

Prine, Virginia Bender. *How Puppies are Born*. New York: Howell, 1972.

PUPPY CARE AND TRAINING

Daglish, E. Fitch. *Care and Training of Your Puppy*. New York: Arco Publishing Co., 1971.

Merriwether, Elizabeth. *Raising Puppies for Pleasure and Profit*. New York: Macmillan, 1970.

Pinkwater, Jill, and Manus, D. *Superpuppy, How to Choose, Raise and Train the Best Possible Dog for You*. New York: Seabury, 1977.

Whiting, Marly. *From Cradle to College*. Minneapolis, no date.

NUTRITION AND FEEDING

Collins, Donald. *The Collins Guide to Dog Nutrition*. New York: Howell, 1972.

Gaines Dog Research Center. *Basic Guide to Canine Nutrition*. White Plains, New York.

Levy, Julliette de Bairacli. *The Complete Herbal Book for the Dog*. New York: Arco Publishing Co., 1971.

McCay, Clive M. *Nutrition of the Dog*. Ithaca: Comstock Publishing Co., 1943.

SOME TECHNICAL BOOKS YOU MAY BE INTERESTED IN

Cohen, J. R., and Fox, Michael W. *How Animals Communicate*. Bloomington: Indiana University Press, 1974.

Fiennes, Richard and Alice. *The Natural History of Dogs*. New York: Bonanza Books, 1968.

Fox, Michael W. *Integrative Development of Brain and Behavior in the Dog*. Chicago: University of Chicago Press, 1971.

Scott, John Paul. *Animal Behavior*. Chicago: University of Chicago Press, 1958.

Scott, John Paul, and Fuller, John L. *Genetics and the Social Behavior of the Dog*. Chicago: University of Chicago Press, 1965.

Skinner, B. F. *The Behavior of Organisms*. New York: Appleton-Century-Crofts, 1938.

DOGS AND
HUMAN DEVELOPMENT

Boone, J. Allen. *Kinship with All Life.* New York: Harper and Row, 1954.

Fox, Michael W. *Between Animal and Man.* New York: Coward, McCann and Geoghegan, 1976.

Levinson, Boris. *Pets and Human Development.* Springfield: Charles C. Thomas, 1972.

———. *Pet-Oriented Child Psychotherapy.* Springfield: Charles C. Thomas, 1969.

STRUCTURE AND MOVEMENT IN THE DOG

The Canine, A Veterinary Aid in Anatomical Transparencies. Grafton, Wisconsin: Fromm Laboratories, 1967.

Elliot, Rachel Page. *Dog Steps, Illustrated Gait at a Glance.* New York: Howell, 1973.

Hollenbeck, Leon. *The Dynamics of Canine Gait.* Akron, New York: Hollenbeck, 1971.

Lyon, McDowell. *The Dog in Action.* New York, Howell, 1966.

Smythe, R. H. *The Conformation of the Dog.* London: Popular Dogs Publishing, 1957.

———. *Dog Structure and Movement.* London: Popular Dogs Publishing, 1970.

SOME ARTICLES ABOUT THE DOG TRAINING AND BREEDING PROGRAMS AT NEW SKETE

Evans, Brother Job. "Dog Psychiatry." *Off Lead* (November 1976), p. 20.

———. "One for the Road: Notes on Roadworking Dogs." *Off Lead* (November 1975), p. 14.

———. "Gone to the Dogs: The German Shepherd Breeding Program at New Skete." *Gleanings* (Winter 1975), p. 15.

———. "Monastery Hosts Search and Rescue Dogs." *Washington County Post,* July 17, 1975, p. 5.

———. "A Puppy Obstacle Course." *Off Lead* (May 1977), p. 10.

———. "Philosophy and Training." *Off Lead* (May 1978).

———. "The Vow of Obedience: The Dog Training Program at New Skete." *Gleanings* (Summer-Fall 1975), p. 15.

Labish, Brother Isaac. "Beware the Dog." *Off Lead* (July 1975), p. 18, and in *Gleanings* (Spring 1974), p. 61.

Marcuso, Sister Teresa. "Midwife for My Dog." *Gleanings* (Spring 1978), p. 54.

Mellon, Robert. "The Brotherhood of Saint Francis." *Adirondack Life* (Spring 1971), p. 48.

Oliver, Sister Magdalene. "The Journey Home." *Gleanings* (Winter 1973), p. 6.

Rendel, John. "Monastery Raising German Shepherds." *The New York Times,* November 30, 1969.

Vanacore, Connie. "The Monks of New Skete." *The American Kennel Club Gazette* (December 1975), p. 24.

PERIODICALS: DOG BEHAVIOR AND TRAINING

Front and Finish. P.O. Box 333, Galesburg, Ill. 61401. Monthly.

Off Lead, the National Dog Training Monthly. P.O. Box 307, Graves Road, Westmoreland, N.Y., 13490. Monthly.

PERIODICALS: GENERAL

The American Kennel Club Gazette. 51 Madison Avenue, New York, N.Y. 10001. Monthly.

Dog World. 10060 West Roosevelt Road, Westchester, Ill. 60153. Monthly.

The Humane Society News. Humane Society of the United States, 2100 L Street, N.W., Washington, D.C. 20037. Quarterly.

Mainstream. The Animal Protection Institute, Box 22505, Sacramento, Calif. 95822. Monthly.

Pet News, the Educational Pet Journal. 44 Court Street, Brooklyn, N.Y. 11201. Monthly.

Schutzhund USA. 3924 Sylvan Avenue, Modesto, Calif. 95355. Bi-monthly.

The World of the Working Dog. P.O. Box 205, Spring Valley, N.Y. 10977. Bi-monthly.

The following dog food companies publish newsletters and other materials that occasionally contain information on behavior and training, especially as it relates to nutrition:

Gaines News. Gaines Dog Research Center, White Plains, N.Y.

Hill's Division, Riviana Foods Inc., Box 148, Topeka, Kans. 66601.

Purina Kennel News. Professional Marketing Services, Ralston Purina Company, Checkerboard Square, Saint Louis, Mo. 63188.

A SPECIAL RECORDING

Dogtalk. Dr. Michael Fox, Life-Lite Concepts, 565 Fifth Ave., New York, N.Y. 10017.

You may want to write to the following publishers and ask for a complete catalog of their books about dogs:

Arner Publications, P.O. Box 307, Graves Road, Westmoreland, N.Y. 13490.

William W. Denlinger's, Box 76, Fairfax, Va. 22030.

Howell Book House, 730 Fifth Avenue, New York, N.Y. 10019.

Index